THE HERITAGE OF AMERICA

by Nancy J. Skarmeas

He who looks with pride upon this history which his fathers have written by their heroic deeds, who accepts with gratitude the inheritance which they have bequeathed to him, and who highly resolves to preserve this inheritance unimpaired and to pass it on to his descendants enlarged and enriched, is a true American, be his birthplace or his percentage what it may.

Rev. Lyman Abbott

IDEALS PUBLICATIONS INCORPORATED
NASHVILLE, TENNESSEE

EDITOR'S NOTE

On the following pages, we have tried to retain the original spelling, punctuation, and grammar of our text selections to give the historical flavor of the author. In addition, we realize that the heritage of America has been, and continues to be, shaped by a diverse mixture of individuals and groups, many of whom are not mentioned on the pages that follow. We have attempted to be as inclusive as possible, but our selections are not meant as a definitive or complete description of the national character, but only as a sampling of that vast and varied heritage shared by all Americans.

ACKNOWLEDGMENTS

THE SPIRIT OF LIBERTY from *THE SPIRIT OF LIBERTY* by Learned Hand, edit., I. Dilliard. Copyright 1952, 1953, © 1959, 1960 by Alfred A Knopf Inc. Reprinted by permission of the publisher. AN IMMIGRANT PEDDLER by Morris Horowitz and THE OREGON TRAIL by Mary Patton Taylor from *FIRST-PERSON AMERICA*, edited by Ann Banks and reissued by Norton in 1993. DOWN THE SANTA FE TRAIL by Susan Shelby Magoffin from *DOWN THE SANTA FE TRAIL: THE DIARY OF SUSAN SHELBY MAGOFFIN 1846–1847*, edited by Stella Drumm, published by Yale University Press, copyright © 1926. THE JOURNAL OF MARGARET MORRIS from *THE JOURNAL OF MARGARET MORRIS*, Arno Press, Inc., copyright © 1969. Permission granted by Ayer Company Publishers. AMERICA'S WELCOME HOME by Henry Van Dyke reprinted by permission of Charles Scribner's Sons, an imprint of Macmillan Publishing Company, from *THE POEMS OF HENRY VAN DYKE*. Copyright 1919, and renewed 1947, by Charles Scribner's Sons. THE AMERICAN IDEA by Theodore H. White copyright © 1986 by The New York Times Company. Reprinted by permission. Our sincere thanks to Dorothy Pittman, whom we were unable to contact for use of A REVOLUTIONARY WAR JOURNAL by Deborah Sampson Gannett.

ART AND PHOTOGRAPHY

Archive Photos: 15, 24, 31, 43, 69, 70, 95, 116, 141. Art Resource/New York: 6, 10, 11, 13, 22, 38, 41, 43, 50, 51, 56, 58, 76, 88, 104, 109, 110, 111, 112, 123, 124, 125, 130, 139, 143, 144, 150. FPG International: 10, 74, 77, 97, 108, 113, 117, 118, 126, 127, 145. Smithsonian Institution: 158, Stars and Stripes, Smithsonian Institution Photo No. 83-7221. Superstock, Inc.: 8, A.K.G. Berlin; 16, New Bedford Public Library/Lerner Collection; 20–21; 35; 36, Yale University, New Haven, CT/A.K.G. Berlin; 44, Museum of Fine Art, Boston/Lerner Collection; 62–63; 65; 72–73; 75, National Gallery of Art, Washington, D.C.; 78–79; 86–87; 90–91; 92–93, Vaga, NY; 94, National Gallery of Art, Washington, D.C.; 99; 100, Brooklyn Museum, New York/Lerner Collection; 106–107, Lerner Collection; 120–121; 129; 132–133; 137, H. Lanks; 138, Smithsonian Institute, Washington D.C./Bridgeman Art Library, London; 148–149; 152; 156–157.

Special thanks to Stephanie E. Allin, Public Affairs Specialist, National Archives, Washington, D.C.

ISBN 0-8249-4059-8

Printed and bound in the United States of America

Published by Ideals Publications Incorporated
565 Marriott Drive
Nashville, TN 37214
Film separations by Precision Color Graphics, New Berlin, WI
Printed and Bound by Arcata Graphics, Hawkins County, TN

CONTENTS

THE STRUGGLE FOR LIBERTY

My country 'tis of thee
Sweet land of liberty;
Of thee I sing:
Land where my fathers died
Land of the pilgrims' pride
From every mountainside
Let freedom ring.

Samuel Francis Smith
from "America"

THE LIBERTY SONG

John Dickinson, 1768

Come join hand in hand brave Americans all,
And rouse your bold hearts at fair Liberty's call;
No tyrannous acts shall suppress your just claim,
Or stain with dishonour America's name.

In Freedom we're born and in Freedom we'll live,
Our purses are ready,
Steady, Friends, Steady.
Not as Slaves, but as Freemen our money we'll give.

Our worthy Forefathers—Let's give them a cheer
To Climates unknown did courageously steer;
Thro' Oceans, to deserts, for freedom they came,
And dying bequeath'd us their freedom and Fame.

Then join hand in hand brave Americans all,
By uniting we stand, by dividing we fall;
In so Righteous a cause let us hope to succeed,
For Heaven approves of each generous deed.

All ages shall speak with amaze and applause,
Of the courage we'll shew in support of our laws;
To die we can bear—but to serve we disdain,
For shame is to Freedom more dreadful than pain.

This bumper I crown for our Sovereign's health,
And this for Britannia's glory and wealth;
That wealth and that glory immortal may be,
If she is but just—and if we are but free.

John Dickinson was a Pennsylvania lawyer with a flair for writing who helped raise the ire of American colonists against the unfair taxation practices of the British crown. Born in 1732, Dickinson first made his name known with Letters from a Farmer in Pennsylvania, *a series of twelve letters written to oppose the Townshend Acts, which increased taxes on the colonists. "The Liberty Song," written in 1768, became a colonial anthem. Its line—"By uniting we stand, by dividing we fall"—helped convince the colonists that there was power in their numbers. Dickinson went on to serve in the Continental Congress and at the Constitutional Convention. He originally opposed the Declaration of Independence, believing that the colonies' differences with Great Britain could be worked out without separation, but eventually came around to support the cause of independence. Dickinson College in Carlisle, Pennsylvania, is named in his honor.*

THE PATRIOTIC AMERICAN FARMER.
J-N D-K-NS—N, Esq; Barrister at Law
Who with Attic Eloquence and Roman Spirit hath afferted the Liberties of the British Colonies in America.

'Tis nobly done to Stem Taxations Rage,
And raise the Thoughts of a degenerate Age,
For Happiness and Joy, from Freedom spring;
But Life in Bondage is a worthless Thing.

RELIEF-CUT RIGHT:
JOHN DICKINSON (1732-1808)
PAUL REVERE (1735-1818)
PUBLISHED IN *AN ASTRONOMICAL DIARY; OR ALMANACK*, 1772
NATIONAL PORTRAIT GALLERY
SMITHSONIAN INSTITUTION

Patrick Henry (1736-1799) was a Virginia lawyer and an outspoken proponent of American independence from Great Britain. First elected to the Virginia legislature in 1763, Henry went on to serve on the Virginia Committee of Correspondence and the Continental Congress. The speech that made him famous—and that made the line "Give me liberty, or give me death!" a permanent part of American legend—was delivered in March of 1775 at St. John's Church in Richmond, Virginia. Henry's aim was to convince the Virginia legislature to arm its militia to fight the British; the result was a surge in patriotism throughout the colonies.

GIVE ME LIBERTY, OR GIVE ME DEATH!

from a Speech to the Second Virginia Convention
Patrick Henry, 1775

It is in vain, sir, to extenuate the matter. Gentlemen may cry peace, peace—but there is no peace. The war is actually begun! The next gale that sweeps from the North will bring to our ears the clash of resounding arms! Our brethren are already in the field! Why stand we here idle? What is it that gentlemen wish? What would they have? Is life so dear, or peace so sweet, as to be purchased at the price of chains and slavery? Forbid it, Almighty God! I know not what course others may take; but as for me, give me liberty, or give me death!

THE BILL OF RIGHTS
1789

1. Congress shall make no law respecting an establishment of religion, or prohibiting the free exercise thereof; or abridging the freedom of speech, or of the press; or the right of the people peaceably to assemble, and to petition the Government for a redress of grievances.

2. A well regulated Militia, being necessary to the security of a free State, the right of the people to keep and bear Arms, shall not be infringed.

3. No Soldier shall, in time of peace, be quartered in any house, without the consent of the Owner, nor in time of war, but in a manner to be prescribed by law.

4. The right of the people to be secure in their persons, houses, papers, and effects, against unreasonable searches and seizures, shall not be violated, and no Warrants shall issue, but upon probable cause, supported by Oath or affirmation, and particularly describing the place to be searched, and the persons or things to be seized.

5. No person shall be held to answer for a capital, or otherwise infamous crime, unless on a presentment or indictment of a Grand Jury, except in cases arising in the land or naval forces, or in the Militia, when in actual service in time of war or public danger; nor shall any person be subject for the same offence to be twice put in jeopardy of life or limb; nor shall be compelled in any criminal case to be a witness against himself, nor be deprived of life, liberty, or property, without due process of law; nor shall private property be taken for public use without just compensation.

6. In all criminal prosecutions, the accused shall enjoy the right to a speedy and public trial, by an impartial jury of the State and district wherein the crime shall have been committed, which district shall have been previously ascertained by law, and to be informed of the nature and cause of the accusation; to be confronted with the witnesses against him; to have compulsory process for obtaining witnesses in his favor; and to have the Assistance of Counsel for his defence.

7. In suits at common law, where the value in controversy shall exceed twenty dollars, the right of trial by jury shall be preserved, and no fact tried by a jury shall be otherwise re-examined in any Court of the United States, than according to the rules of the common law.

8. Excessive bail shall not be required, nor excessive fines imposed, nor cruel and unusual punishments inflicted.

9. The enumeration in the Constitution, of certain rights, shall not be construed to deny or disparage others retained by the people.

10. The powers not delegated to the United States by the Constitution, nor prohibited by it to the States, are reserved to the States respectively, or to the people.

PAINTING OPPOSITE:
The Spirit of '76
ARCHIBALD M. WILLARD

ENGRAVING ABOVE:
PAUL REVERE'S RIDE
FPG INTERNATIONAL

Listen, my children, and you shall hear
Of the midnight ride of Paul Revere,
On the eighteenth of April, in Seventy-five;
Hardly a man is now alive
Who remembers that famous day and year.

He said to his friend, "If the British march
By land or sea from the town tonight,
Hang a lantern aloft in the belfry arch
Of the North Church tower
    as a signal light,—
One, if by land, and two, if by sea;
And I on the opposite shore will be,
Ready to ride and spread the alarm
Through every Middlesex village and farm,
For the country folk to be up and to arm."

Henry Wadsworth Longfellow
from "Paul Revere's Ride"

PAINTING BELOW:
THE CONTINENTALS
FRANK BLACKWELL MAYER
GEORGE BUCHANAN COALE COLLECTION
NATIONAL MUSEUM OF AMERICAN ART
SMITHSONIAN INSTITUTION

The God who gave us life, gave us liberty at the same time.

Thomas Jefferson
*Summary of the Rights
of British America*

God grants liberty only to those who love it, and are always ready to guard and defend it.

Daniel Webster

In giving freedom to the slave, we assure freedom to the free, honorable alike in what we give and what we preserve.

Abraham Lincoln

We wish that this column, rising towards heaven among the pointed spires of so many temples dedicated to God, may contribute also to produce in all minds a pious feeling of dependence and gratitude. We wish, finally, that the last object to the sight of him who leaves his native shore, and the first to gladden he who revisits it, may be something which shall remind him of the liberty and glory of his country. Let it rise! let it rise, till it meet the sun in his coming; let the earliest light of the morning gild it, and the parting day linger and play on its summit!

Daniel Webster, 1825
*Address on the dedication of
the Bunker Hill Monument,*

Charlotte Perkins Gilman's work Women and Economics, *published in 1898, is considered a classic in the history of women's fight for equal rights and liberty in American society. Gilman, an author of poetry and short stories as well as editor of the leading feminist magazine* Forerunner, *overcame a difficult childhood as well as psychological problems in her youth to become one of the most respected voices in the movement to secure equal rights for women.*

PORTRAIT ABOVE:
CHARLOTTE PERKINS GILMAN (1860-1935)
ELLEN DAY HALE (1855-1940)
OIL ON PANEL
NATIONAL PORTRAIT GALLERY
SMITHSONIAN INSTITUTION

PHOTOGRAPH BELOW:
WOMEN'S SUFFRAGE PARADE,
MARCH 3, 1913, WASHINGTON, D. C.
LIBRARY OF CONGRESS

In conclusion, then, let us say, in behalf of the women of this State, we ask for all that you have asked for yourselves in the progress of your development, since the *Mayflower* cast anchor beside Plymouth rock; and simply on the ground that the rights of every human being are the same and identical.

Elizabeth Cady Stanton
*Address to the Legislature
of New York
on Women's Rights, 1854*

STANZAS FOR THE TIMES

John Greenleaf Whittier, 1835

Is this the land our fathers loved,
   The freedom which they toiled to win?
Is this the soil whereon they moved?
   Are these the graves they slumber in?
Are we the sons by whom are borne
The mantles which the dead have worn? . . .

Shall outraged Nature cease to feel?
   Shall Mercy's tears no longer flow?
Shall ruffian threats of cord and steel—
   The dungeon's gloom—the assassin's blow,
Turn back the spirit roused to save
The Truth, our Country, and the Slave? . . .

What! shall we guard our neighbor still,
   While woman shrieks beneath his rod,
And while he tramples down at will
   The image of a common God?
Shall watch and ward be round him set,
Of Northern nerve and bayonet?

And shall we know and share with him
   The danger and the growing shame?
And see our Freedom's light grow dim,
   Which should have filled
the world with flame!
And, writhing, feel, where'er we turn,
A world's reproach around us burn?

Is't not enough that this is borne?
   And asks our haughty neighbor more?
Must fetters which his slaves have worn,
   Clank round the Yankee farmer's door?
Must he be told, beside his plough,
What he must speak, and when, and how?

Must he be told his freedom stands
   On Slavery's dark foundations strong—
On breaking hearts and fettered hands,
   On robbery, and crime, and wrong?
That all his fathers taught is vain—
That Freedom's emblem is the chain? . . .

Rail on, then, "brethren of the South"—
   Ye shall not hear the truth the less—
No seal is on the Yankee's mouth,
   No fetter on the Yankee press!
From our Green Mountains to the Sea,
One voice shall thunder—WE ARE FREE!

"Stanzas for the Times" was poet John Greenleaf Whittier's response to proposed restrictions on free speech aimed at quieting the abolitionist movement. Whittier, a Massachusetts Quaker, was an outspoken leader in the anti-slavery cause; he refused to be silenced or appeased until the goal of freedom for Americans of all races was won. Besides his work for abolition, Whittier is known for writing traditional American poems.

PAINTING LEFT: [18.393]
WOUNDED DRUMMER BOY
WILLIAM MORRIS HUNT
(1824-1879)
OIL ON CANVAS
14 x 19¼ INCHES
GIFT FROM THE ISAAC FENNO
COLLECTION
MUSEUM OF FINE ARTS
BOSTON, MASSACHUSETTS

ADDRESS TO THE OHIO WOMEN'S RIGHTS CONVENTION
Sojourner Truth, 1851

Well, children, where there is so much racket there must be something out of kilter. I think that twixt the Negroes of the South and the women at the North, all talking about rights, the white men will be in a fix pretty soon. But what's all this here talking about?

That man over there says that women need to be helped into carriages, and lifted over ditches, and to have the best place everywhere. Nobody ever helps me into carriages, or over mud puddles, or gives me any best place! And ain't I a woman? Look at me! Look at my arm! I have ploughed and planted, and gathered into barns, and no man could head me! And ain't I a woman? I could work as much and eat as much as a man—when I could get it—and bear the lash as well! And ain't I a woman? I have borne thirteen children, and seen them most all sold off to slavery, and when I cried out with my mother's grief, none but Jesus heard me! And ain't I a woman?

Then they talk about this thing in the head; what's this they call it? . . . That's it, honey. What's that got to do with women's rights or Negro's rights? If my cup won't hold but a pint, and yours holds a quart, wouldn't you be mean not to let me have my little half-measure full?

Then that little man in black there, he says that women can't have as much rights as men, 'cause Christ wasn't a woman! Where did your Christ come from? Where did your Christ come from? From God and a woman! Man had nothing to do with Him.

If the first woman God ever made was strong enough to turn the world upside down all alone, these women together ought to be able to turn it back, and get it right side up again! And now they is asking to do it, the men better let them.

Obliged to you for hearing me, and now old Sojourner ain't got nothing more to say.

I SELL THE SHADOW TO SUPPORT THE SUBSTANCE.
SOJOURNER TRUTH.

Randall

East Grand Circus Park,
DETROIT.

Sojourner Truth was born into slavery in Ulster County, New York, around 1797. Given the name Isabella, she lived out her childhood and early adulthood as a slave before gaining her freedom sometime in the 1830s. A free woman, Isabella traveled to New York City where she worked as a paid domestic servant and became involved with local evangelical Christians. In 1843 Isabella renamed herself Sojourner Truth and set out on the road to preach about the love of God. A powerful, compelling speaker, Sojourner began to draw crowds and soon added abolition and women's rights to her mission. She spoke at the very first National Woman's Rights Convention in Worcester, Massachusetts, in 1850, and the next year, at the convention in Ohio. Many at first objected to her presence, fearing that the cause of women's rights would become inseparable in the public mind from that of abolition, but all who heard her speak agreed that hers was a voice that must be heard. In 1864 Sojourner Truth's contribution to American liberty was acknowledged by President Lincoln, who invited her to the White House.

PHOTO LEFT:
SOJOURNER TRUTH (1797?-1883)
RANDALL STUDIO
NATIONAL PORTRAIT GALLERY
SMITHSONIAN INSTITUTION

A DISAPPOINTED WOMAN

Lucy Stone, 1885

The last speaker alluded to this movement as being that of a few disappointed women. From the first years to which my memory stretches, I have been a disappointed woman. When, with my brothers, I reached forth after the sources of knowledge, I was reproved with "It isn't fit for you; it doesn't belong to women." Then there was but one college in the world where women were admitted, and that was in Brazil. I would have found my way there, but by the time I was prepared to go, one was opened in the young State of Ohio—the first in the United States where women and Negroes could enjoy opportunities with white men. I was disappointed when I came to seek a profession worthy an immortal being—every employment was closed to me, except those of the teacher, the seamstress, and the housekeeper. In education, in marriage, in religion, in everything, disappointment is the lot of woman. It shall be the business of my life to deepen this disappointment in every woman's heart until she bows down to it no longer. I wish that women, instead of being walking show-cases, instead of begging of their fathers and brothers the latest and gayest new bonnet, would ask of them their rights.

The question of Woman's Rights is a practical one. The notion has prevailed that it was only an ephemeral idea; that it was but women claiming the right to smoke cigars in the streets, and to frequent bar-rooms. Others have supposed it a question of comparative intellect; others still, of sphere. Too much has already been said and written about woman's sphere. Trace all the doctrines to their source and they will be found to have no basis except in the usages and prejudices of the age. This is seen in the fact that what is tolerated in woman in one country is not tolerated in another. . . . Wendell Phillips says, "The best and greatest thing one is capable of doing, that is his sphere." I have confidence in the Father to believe that when He gives us the capacity to do anything He does not make a blunder. Leave women, then, to find their sphere. And do not tell us before we are born even, that our province is to cook dinners, darn stockings, and sew on buttons. . . .

"A Disappointed Woman" is from a speech delivered by Lucy Stone at a women's rights convention in Ohio in 1855. Stone, born in Massachusetts, went against her family's wishes to attend Oberlin College in Ohio and again defied tradition after her marriage by keeping her own name. With her husband, Henry Blackwell, Stone wrote a marriage contract that denied the subjugation of wife to husband. In every facet of her life, Lucy Stone worked to promote liberty for women in a society where the majority of men, and women, shared the fears of the creator of this cartoon that women's rights and women's suffrage would have frightening consequences for the American family.

CARTOON RIGHT:
ELECTION DAY!
E. W. GUSTON, 1909
LIBRARY OF CONGRESS

PHOTOGRAPH ABOVE:
WOMEN MARCHERS
ARCHIVE PHOTOS/HACKETT COLLECTION

Although Americans proudly date their national liberty to the end of the Revolutionary War, true liberty for all Americans has been in many cases slow to follow. The Nineteenth Amendment, guaranteeing the vote to women, was not passed until February 27, 1922. The amendment was first introduced to Congress by Senator Aaron A. Sargent of California in 1878. It was defeated that year, and every following year, until its passage nearly half a century later.

AMERICA

Samuel Francis Smith, 1832

My country 'tis of thee
Sweet land of liberty;
    Of thee I sing.
Land where my fathers died
Land of the pilgrims' pride
From every mountainside
    Let freedom ring.

My native country—thee
Land of the noble free,
    Thy name I love;
I love thy rocks and rills
Thy woods and templed hills
My heart with rapture thrills
    Like that above.

Let music swell the breeze
And ring from all the trees
    Sweet freedom's song
Let mortal tongues awake
Let all that breathe partake
Let rocks their silence break
    The sound prolong.

Our fathers' God, to thee
Author of liberty
    To thee we sing
Long may our land be bright
With freedom's holy light;
Protect us by Thy might,
    Great God, our King.

THE SPIRIT OF LIBERTY

Judge Learned Hand

from a speech delivered May 21, 1944, on "I Am an American Day" in New York City

What then is the spirit of liberty? I cannot define it; I can only tell you of my own faith. The spirit of liberty is the spirit which is not too sure that it is right; the spirit of liberty is the spirit which seeks to understand the minds of other men and women; the spirit of liberty is the spirit which weighs their interests alongside its own without bias; the spirit of liberty remembers that not even a sparrow falls to earth unheeded; the spirit of liberty is the spirit of Him who, near two thousand years ago, taught mankind that lesson it has never learned, but has never quite forgotten; that there may be a kingdom where the least shall be heard and considered side by side with the greatest. And now in that spirit, that spirit of an America which has never been, and which may never be; nay, which never will be except as the conscience and courage of Americans create it; yet in the spirit of that America which lies hidden in some form in the aspirations of us all; in the spirit of that America for which our young men are at this moment fighting and dying; in that spirit of liberty and of America I ask you to rise and with me pledge our faith in the glorious destiny of our beloved country.

PAINTING ABOVE:
THE COUNTY ELECTION (1851-52)
GEORGE CALEB BINGHAM (1811-1879)
THE ST. LOUIS ART MUSEUM
ST. LOUIS, MISSOURI

OUR
HERITAGE
OF COURAGE

Not gold but only men can make
A people great and strong;
Men who for truth and honor's sake
Stand fast and suffer long.

Brave men who work while others sleep,
Who dare while others fly—
They build a nation's pillars deep
And lift them to the sky.

Ralph Waldo Emerson
from "A Nation's Strength"

PAINTING RIGHT: [48.456]
NIAGARA FALLS FROM TABLE ROCK, C.1801-02
JOHN F. VANDERLYN (1775-1852)
OIL ON CANVAS
24 X 30 INCHES
BEQUEST OF MARTHA C. KAROLIK FOR THE
KAROLIK COLLECTION OF AMERICAN PAINTINGS
MUSEUM OF FINE ARTS
BOSTON, MASSACHUSETTS

THE MAYFLOWER COMPACT
1620

In the name of God Amen. We whose names are underwritten, the loyall subjects of our dread soveraigne Lord King James by the grace of God, of great Britaine, Franc, and Ireland king, defender of the faith, &c.

Haveing undertaken, for the glorie of God, and advancements of the Christian faith and honour of our king & countrie, a voyage to plant the first colonie in the Northerne parts of Virginia, doe by these presents solemnly & mutualy in the presence of God, and one another, covenant & combine our selves togeather into a civill body politick; for our better ordering, & preservation & furtherance of the ends aforesaid; and by vertue hereof to enacte, constitute, and frame shuch just & equall lawes, ordinances, Acts, constitutions, & offices, from time to time, as shall be thought most meete & convenient for the generall good of the Colonie: unto which we promise all due submission and obedience.

In witnes whereof we have hereunder subscribed our names at Cap-Codd the 11 of November, in the year of the raign of our soveraign Lord King James of England, France, & Ireland, the eighteenth and of Scotland the fiftie fourth. An. Dom. 1620.

PAINTING ABOVE:
THE EMBARCATION OF THE PILGRIMS
ROBERT W. WEIR (1803-1889)

The Mayflower set sail across the Atlantic carrying 102 passengers with the intention of settling in territory controlled by the Virginia Company of London. When they found themselves instead landing a good distance north at Cape Cod, Massachusetts, on land beyond the borders controlled by their countrymen, the passengers agreed to sign a covenant guaranteeing government by law, by the consent of the governed. The Mayflower Compact, signed by fifty-one of the ship's male passengers in November of 1620, established self-rule for what would be known as the Plymouth Colony. Only about a third of the Mayflower's passengers were members of the English separatist group called Pilgrims; others came simply seeking new opportunities and new life in America. In time, however, the entire colony would be known by the name of Pilgrims, and their courage and perseverance would become a cherished and celebrated part of our American heritage.

THE AMERICAN CRISIS

Thomas Paine, 1776

These are the times that try men's souls. The summer soldier and the sunshine patriot will, in this crisis, shrink from the service of his country; but he that stands it NOW, deserves the love and thanks of man and woman. Tyranny, like hell, is not easily conquered; yet we have this consolation with us, that the harder the conflict, the more glorious the triumph. What we obtain too cheap, we esteem too lightly; 'tis dearness only that gives every thing its value. Heaven knows how to put a proper price upon its goods; and it would be strange indeed, if so celestial an article as FREEDOM should not be highly rated.

ENGRAVING RIGHT:
THOMAS PAINE (1737-1809)
JAMES WATSON
NATIONAL PORTRAIT GALLERY
SMITHSONIAN INSTITUTION

COMMON SENSE

Thomas Paine, 1776

But where, say some, is the king of America? I'll tell you, friend, he reigns above, and doth not make havoc of mankind like the Royal Brute of Great Britain. Yet that we may not appear to be defective even in earthly honors, let a day be solemnly set apart for proclaiming the charter; let it be brought forth placed upon the divine law, the Word of God; let a crown be placed thereon, by which the world may know, that so far as we approve of monarchy, that in America THE LAW IS KING. For as in absolute governments the king is law, so in free countries the law ought to be king, and there ought to be no other. But lest any ill use should afterwards arise, let the crown at the conclusion of the ceremony be demolished, and scattered among the people whose right it is. . . .

O ye that love mankind! Ye that dare oppose not only the tyranny but the tyrant, stand forth! Every spot of the old world is overrun with oppression. Freedom hath been hunted round the globe. Asia and Africa have long expelled her. Europe regards her like a stranger, and England hath given her warning to depart. O receive the fugitive, and prepare in time an asylum for mankind.

Thomas Paine was a passionate, outspoken, courageous, and always controversial leader in the cause of American independence. Born in 1737, Paine came to prominence in 1776 with the publication of the first in a series of sixteen pamphlets he called "The American Crisis." The pamphlets, bearing the signature "Common Sense" rather than the name of the author, argued that fighting against taxation was not enough—Americans must demand complete and total independence. Paine's pamphlets sold close to 500,000 copies and helped stir the colonists to action. After American independence was secured, Paine traveled to France, where he championed the French Revolution, but was eventually exiled for his defense of the life of the ousted king. He will be forever remembered in American history as one of the boldest and most courageous champions of independence.

from A REVOLUTIONARY WAR JOURNAL

Deborah Sampson Gannett

Later in June, Sampson and thirty other soldiers volunteered at the Point to flush out armed Tories in East Chester. Early one morning, while it was still dark and they were encamped at a place called Vonhoite, guard pickets sounded the alarm at the approach of mounted, armed men. Silence was shattered by a barrage of gunfire. When the air cleared, several Tories and one Continental soldier had died. Deborah Sampson was among the wounded. "I considered this as a death wound, or as being equivalent to it; as it must, I thought, lead to the discovery of my sex. Covered with blood from head to foot, I told my companions I fear I had received a mortal wound; and I begged them to leave me to die on the spot: preferring to take the small chance I should in this case have of surviving, rather than to be carried to the hospital. To this my comrades would not consent; but one of them took me before him on his horse, and in this painful manner I was borne six miles to the hospital of the French army, at a place called Crompond. On coming in sight of the hospital, my heart again failed me. In a paroxysm of despair, I actually drew a pistol from the holster, and was about to put an end to my life. That I did not proceed to the fatal act, I can ascribe only to the interposition of Divine Mercy.

"The French surgeon, on my being brought in, instantly came. He was alert, cheerful, humane. 'How you lose so much blood at this early hour? Be any bone broken?' . . . My head having been bound up, and a change of clothing becoming a wounded soldier being ready, I was asked by the too inquisitive French surgeon whether I had any other wound. He had observed my extreme paleness, and that I limped in attempting to walk. I readily replied in the negative: it was a plump falsehood! 'Sit you down my lad; your boot say you fib!' said the surgeon, noticing that the blood still oozed from it. He took off my boots and stockings with his own hands with great tenderness, and washed my leg to the knee. I then told him I would retire, change my clothing, and if any other wound should appear, I would inform him.

"Meanwhile, I had procured in the hospital a silver probe a little curved at the end, a needle, some lint, a bandage, and some of the same kind of salve that had been applied to the wound in my head. I found that the ball had penetrated my thigh about two inches, and the wound was still moderately bleeding. The wine had revived me, and God, by his kind care, watched over me. At the third attempt I extracted the ball.

"This operation over, the blood was staunched, and my regimentals, stiff enough to stand alone, had been exchanged for a loose, thin wrapper, when I was again visited by the surgeon. In his watchful eye I plainly read doubts. . . . I had less dread of receiving half a dozen more balls than the penetrating glance of his eye. As I grew better his scrutiny diminished.

"Before the wound in my thigh was half healed, I rejoined the army on the lines. But had the most hardy soldier been in the condition I was when I left the hospital, he would have been excused from military duty.

Deborah Sampson Gannett was a colonial woman determined to fight for the cause of American independence. Twice, dressed as a man, she enlisted in the Continental Army. The first time, her gender was discovered; the second, she successfully joined and fought. Her original journal was lost, but she recounted many of her experiences to a writer who assisted her in recreating her journal. Her story is a lasting record of a unique brand of courage and patriotism.

The Mayflower *was just one of countless ships that carried settlers to new lives in America. The bravery of these immigrants cannot be exaggerated: facing a treacherous ocean crossing, an untamed wilderness with a harsh climate, and complete separation from home, family, and everything familiar, these courageous men and women are the true foundation of the America we know and love today.*

PAINTING LEFT:
ARRIVAL OF THE FIRST PERMANENT ENGLISH SETTLERS
LIBRARY OF CONGRESS

The battle, sir, is not to the strong alone; it is to the vigilant, the active, the brave. Besides, sir, we have no election. If we were base enough to desire it, it is now too late to retire from the contest. There is no retreat but in submission and slavery! Our chains are forged! Their clanking may be heard on the plains of Boston! The war is inevitable—and let it come! I repeat it, sir, let it come!

Patrick Henry
Speech to the Second Virginia Convention, 1775

PHOTO ABOVE:
UNION SOLDIERS
ARCHIVE PHOTOS/AMERICAN STOCK

I *will be* as harsh as truth, and as uncompromising as justice. . . . I am in earnest—I will not equivocate—I will not excuse—I will not retreat a single inch—AND I WILL BE HEARD.

William Lloyd Garrison
The Liberator

Brethren, arise, arise! Strike for your lives and liberties. Now is the day and the hour. Let every slave throughout the land do this, and the days of slavery are numbered. You cannot be more oppressed than you have been—you cannot suffer greater cruelties than you have already. *Rather die freemen than live to be slaves.* Remember that you are FOUR MILLIONS! . . .

Let your motto be resistance! *resistance!* RESISTANCE! No oppressed people have ever secured their liberty without resistance. What kind of resistance you had better make you must decide by the circumstances that surround you, and according to the suggestion of expediency. Brethren, adieu! Trust in the living God. Labor for the peace of the human race, and remember that you are FOUR MILLIONS!

Henry Highland Garnet
Call to Rebellion, 1843

POSTER BELOW:
WASTE HELPS THE ENEMY
VANDERLAAN
PHOTOLITHOGRAPH
NATIONAL ARCHIVES

Henry Highland Garnet was the first black clergyman to speak to the United States House of Representatives. Garnet, born a slave in Maryland, escaped captivity at the age of nine and fled to New York. A leader in the abolition movement, Garnet believed that, by 1843, the time for words had passed and the time for action was at hand. He called on those held in slavery in America to band together and win their freedom—with force if necessary. Garnet's courage was an inspiration to many, and his leadership speeded the end of slavery in America.

POSTER RIGHT:
CAN ALL YOU CAN
1943
PHOTOLITHOGRAPH
NATIONAL ARCHIVES

"Use it up, wear it out, make it do, or do without" was a popular saying in the 1940s, when World War II demanded that Americans conserve food, gasoline, and other items. Most Americans readily complied with rationing measures, glad to do something to help their country and their friends and family who were fighting in the war. The courage of those at home, as always, was as vital to the nation as the bravery of the troops in the field.

THE STAR-SPANGLED BANNER

Francis Scott Key, 1814

O say, can you see, by the dawn's early light,
What so proudly we hail'd at the twilight's last gleaming?
Whose broad stripes and bright stars, thro' the perilous fight,
O'er the ramparts we watched, were so gallantly streaming?
And the rocket's red glare, the bombs bursting in air
Gave proof thro' the night that our flag was still there:
O say, does that star-spangled banner yet wave
O'er the land of the free and the home of the brave.

On the shore dimly seen thro' the mists of the deep,
Where the foe's haughty host in dread silence reposes,
What is that which the breeze, o'er the towering steep,
As it fitfully blows, half conceals, half discloses?
Now it catches the gleam of the morning's first beam,
In full glory reflected now shines in the stream.
'Tis the star-spangled banner; O long may it wave
O'er the land of the free and the home of the brave.

And where is the band who so vauntingly swore,
'Mid the havoc of war and the battle's confusion,
A home and a country they'd leave us no more?
Their blood has wash'd out their foul footstep's pollution.
No refuge could save the hireling and slave
From the terror of flight or the gloom of the grave;
And the star-spangled banner in triumph doth wave
O'er the land of the free and the home of the brave.

O thus be it ever, when free men shall stand
Between their loved homes and the war's desolation;
Blest with vict'ry and peace, may the heav'n rescued land
Praise the Power that hath made and preserved us a nation!
Then conquer we must, when our cause it is just,
And this be our motto, "In God is our trust!"
And the star-spangled banner in triumph shall wave
O'er the land of the free and the home of the brave.

PAINTING ABOVE: [03.1079]
THE PASSAGE OF THE DELAWARE, 181
THOMAS SULLY (1783-1872)
OIL ON CANVAS,
146½ X 207 INCHES
MUSEUM OF FINE ARTS
BOSTON, MASSACHUSETTS

George Washington and "The Star-Spangled Banner" are two of our nation's greatest symbols of courage. Washington led the Continental Army against the best trained and strongest forces in the world and then, as our first president, led the fledgling nation in its first bold steps as an independent member of the world community. It is the courage of George Washington and the countless others who have led our nation in times of war and in times of peace that the stirring lines of our national anthem—recognized throughout the world as a statement of American pride and courage—commemorates.

LETTER FROM A CIVIL WAR SOLDIER

George W. Harvey, April 10, 1864

Dear Ana, It is again Sunday, and we have gone through with our weekly inspection. I know of no way in which I can spend my time so agreeably as in writing to loved ones at home. . . .We have had one of the most torrential rains since yesterday morning since I have been in Virginia. . . . It has stopped raining this morning, sun shines out part of the time; but I think the wet weather is not yet over. There will be no moving of the army until we have some dry weather to dry up the mud. . . .You must keep of good courage, Ana. I know that it requires a good deal of fortitude to sustain one in your place. I deeply sympathize with you. I know your anxiety as on one hand you see your parents about to depart for the spiritland, and on the other, a husband and two sons in the army exposed to the horrors of war. I cannot, I would not, say to you do not feel bad, for it is contrary to your true and undying love to your dear husband and your maternal love for your children not to feel bad in a time like this; but I will say try and keep up as good courage as you can. Do not look on the dark side alone. Remember the darkest time is just before day. We

must put our trust in our heavenly Father, hoping that the day star of peace will soon dawn on our land and that we shall all meet again. . . . When I see those slave mothers fleeing from bondage with their little children pressed to their bosoms and see little children with scarcely clothing enough to cover their nakedness, weary with their long marches by night through the roads and see the joy that lights up their countenances when they feel that they are safe within our lines, that they are free, that their children are not to be torn from their fond embrace, I feel that we are engaged in a holy cause, one that God will bless and prosper. I will write to you again in a few days.

Your affectionate husband,

PHOTOGRAPH RIGHT:
*LETTERS BETWEEN
GEORGE HARVEY AND
HIS FAMILY*

George W. Harvey was a forty-three-year-old farmer living in Brattleboro, Vermont, when he enlisted in the Union Army on December 17, 1863. His sons, Nahan, fifteen, and Milo, seventeen, joined the fight along with their father. The Harveys were assigned to the Third Regiment of the Vermont Infantry Volunteers and joined the Grand Army of the Republic at their winter quarters near Brandy Station, Virginia. George Harvey's letter to his wife, at left, reveals a side of war far removed from the great issues and battles and generals. The simple words of George Harvey to his wife express the true depths of courage of each and every man, woman, and child who has made a personal sacrifice for the greater good of our country. Harvey was killed in the Battle of Cold Harbor on June 3, 1864.

PHOTOGRAPH ABOVE:
MT. RUSHMORE, SOUTH DAKOTA

Our nation's many monuments remind us every day of our common heritage of courage. The faces carved into the rock at Mt. Rushmore pay tribute to four of our nation's greatest leaders: George Washington, Thomas Jefferson, Theodore Roosevelt, and Abraham Lincoln. The example of such courageous leaders inspires succeeding generations to stand firmly for themselves, their families, their communities, and their country.

A NATION'S STRENGTH

Ralph Waldo Emerson

What makes a nation's pillars high
And its foundations strong?
What makes it mighty to defy
The foes that round it throng?

It is not gold. Its kingdoms grand
Go down in battle shock;
Its shafts are laid in sinking sand,
Not on abiding rock.

Is it the sword? Ask the red dust
Of empires passed away;
The blood has turned their stones to rust,
Their glory to decay.

And is it pride? Ah, that bright crown
Has seemed to nations sweet;
But God has struck its luster down
In ashes at his feet.

Not gold but only men can make
A people great and strong;
Men who for truth and honor's sake
Stand fast and suffer long.

Brave men who work while others sleep,
Who dare while others fly—
They build a nation's pillars deep
And lift them to the sky.

THE RIGHT IS MORE PRECIOUS THAN PEACE

War Message to Congress, April 2, 1917
Woodrow Wilson

It is a fearful thing to lead this great peaceful people into war. . . . But the right is more precious than peace, and we shall fight for the things which we have always carried nearest our hearts,— for democracy, for the right of those who submit to authority to have a voice in their own Governments, for the rights and liberties of small nations, for a universal dominion of right by such a concert of free peoples as shall bring peace and safety to all nations and make the world itself at last free. To such a task we can dedicate our lives and our fortunes, everything that we are and everything that we have, with the pride of those who know that the day has come when America is privileged to spend her blood and her might for the principles that gave her birth and happiness and the peace which she has treasured. God helping her, she can do no other.

President Woodrow Wilson led the United States into World War I reluctantly but confidently, with the courage of a leader who believed that his actions were in the best interests of his country and the world, and understood that great sacrifices are often necessary in the name of truth and freedom. Wilson's decision signaled not only a new direction for the war, but a new era in international relations— an era that would see the United States of America looked to by nations across the globe for leadership and protection.

Abraham Lincoln stood out at a time in American history when few had the courage to take the bold steps necessary to save our Union. With passions flaring in both the North and the South and the issue of slavery tearing apart the very fabric of our young nation, President Lincoln never lost sight of what he saw as his most sacred duty: preserving the Union. His courage and sacrifice in doing so have made him one of our most beloved and inspirational historical figures.

PHOTO RIGHT:
ABRAHAM LINCOLN IN A CIVIL WAR CAMP
ARCHIVE PHOTOS/HIRZ

OUR LEGACY OF INDEPENDENCE

Whoso would be a man, must be a nonconformist. He who would gather immortal palms must not be hindered by the name of goodness, but must explore if it be goodness. Nothing is at last sacred but the integrity of your own mind. Absolve you to yourself, and you shall have the suffrage of the world.

Ralph Waldo Emerson
from Self-Reliance

Painting above: [48.445]
Fresh Water Cove from Dolliver's Neck, Gloucester, Early 1850s
Fitz Hugh Lane (1804-1865)
Oil on canvas, 24 x 36 inches
Bequest of Martha C. Karolik for the
M. and M. Karolik Collection of American Paintings, 1815-1865
Museum of Fine Arts
Boston, Massachusetts

BOAST NOT PROUD ENGLISH OF THY BIRTH

Roger Williams, 1634

Boast not proud English, of thy birth and blood,
Thy brother Indian is by birth as Good.
Of one blood God made Him, and Thee and All,
As wise, as faire, as strong, as personall.

By nature wrath's his portion, thine no more
Till Grace his soule and thine in Christ restore
Make sure thy second birth, else thou shalt see,
Heaven ope to Indians wild, but shut to thee.

Roger Williams, born in London around 1603, arrived in the Massachusetts Bay Colony in 1631 and almost immediately became a leader in the church at Salem. Just as quickly, however, Williams fell out of favor with the Puritan leaders of the colony for his outspoken views. Williams believed that the New England colonists must declare their complete separation from the Church of England if they hoped to found a new, purer church in the New World. Puritan leaders strongly disagreed, seeing themselves rather as an outpost of the church. Williams left Salem for a time to minister at Plymouth, Massachusetts, an openly separatist settlement. Even there, however, he could not find satisfaction; and he returned to Salem where, by 1635, he was banished forever from Massachusetts for his continuing demands that the churches of New England formally separate from the Church of England and for his statements, which were considered outrageous at the time, that the colonists had no right to the land they had settled until they purchased it from the native inhabitants. Williams, banished in October of 1635, traveled south to the Narragansett country, where he founded Providence, Rhode Island. Years later, Williams became a Baptist but eventually found himself dissatisfied with that faith. A true independent spirit and a man of great courage, Williams in later life referred to himself as a "seeker," one on a perpetual search for truth.

LEFT:
*LEYDEN STREET,
PLYMOUTH, MASSACHUSETTS
LIBRARY OF CONGRESS*

ARGUMENTS FOR RELIGIOUS TOLERATION

Roger Williams, 1655

First, that the blood of so many hundred thousand soules of Protestants and papists, split in the wars of present and former ages, for their respective consciences, is not required nor accepted by Jesus Christ, the Prince of Peace. . . .

It is the will and command of God, that (since the coming of his son the Lord Jesus) a permission of the most paganish, Jewish, Turkish, or antichristian consciences and worships be granted to all men in all nations or countries; and they are only to be fought against with that sword which is only able to conquer, to wit, the sword of God's spirit, the word, of God. . . . God requireth not an uniformity of religion to be inacted or enforced in any civil state; which enforced uniformity (sooner or later) is the greatest occasion of civil war, ravishing of conscience, persecution of Christ Jesus in his servants, and of the hypocrisy and destruction of millions of souls. . . . true civility and Christianity may both flourish in a state or kingdom, notwithstanding the permission of diverse and contrary consciences. . . .

from THE JOURNAL OF MADAM KNIGHT

Sarah Kemble Knight, 1704

Thus, absolutely lost in Thought, and dying with the very thoughts of drowning, I come up with the post, who I did not see till even with his Hors[e]: he told me he stopped for mee; and wee Rode on Very deliberately a few paces, when we entered a Thickett of Trees and Shrubbs, and I perceived by the Hors[e]'s going, we were on the descent of a Hill, which, as wee come neerer the bottom, 'twas totaly dark with the Trees that surrounded it. But I knew by the Going of the Hors[e] wee had entered the water, which my Guide told mee was the hazzardos River he had told me off; and hee, Riding up close to my Side, Bid me not fear— we should be over Imediatly. I now ralyed all the Courage I was mistriss of, Knowing that I must either Venture my fate of drowning, or be left like ye Children in the wood. So, as the Post bid me, I gave Reins to my Nagg; and sitting as Stedy as Just before in the Cannoe, in a few minutes got safe to the other side, which hee told mee was the Narragansett country.

Here We found great difficulty in Travailing, the way being very narrow, and on each side the Trees and bushes gave us very unpleasant welcomes with their Branches and bows, which wee could not avoid, it being so exceeding dark. My Guide, as before so now, putt on harder than I, with my weary bones, could follow; so left mee and the way beehind him. Now Returned my distressed aprehensions of the place where I was: the dolesome woods, my Company next to none, Going I knew not whither, and encompassed with Terrifying darkness; the least of which was enough to startle a more Masculine courage. Added to which the Reflections, as in the afternoon of yesterday that my Call was very Questionable, which till then I had not so Prudently as I ought considered. Now, coming to the foot of a hill, I found great difficulty in ascending; But being got to the Top, was there amply recompenced with the friendly Appearance of the Kind Conductress of the night, Just then Advancing above the Horisontall Line. The Raptures which the Sight of that fair Planett produced in mee caus'd mee, for the Moment, to forgett my present wearyness and past toils. . . .

Sarah Kemble Knight (1666-1727) was an oddity in colonial America—an independent businesswoman. One of her first ventures was a writing school in New York City, which offered instruction to, among others, Benjamin Franklin. Her journal, first printed in 1825, tells the story of a trip on horseback from Boston to New York City in the fall of 1704 to look after business matters. A difficult journey by any account, it was one unheard of for an unescorted woman of the day. Mrs. Knight's journal is not only a colorful depiction of the manners, customs, and countryside of colonial America but also a tribute to an independent woman who, at a time when women's rights were taken seriously by no more than a handful of colonists, simply did what she wanted and needed to do without regard to prevailing prejudices.

PAINTING ABOVE:
HER WEIGHT IN GOLD
J. L. G. FERRIS (1863-1930)

PAINTING ABOVE:
SIGNING OF THE DECLARATION
OF INDEPENDENCE
JOHN TRUMBULL (1756-1843)

THE DECLARATION OF INDEPENDENCE
1776

When in the Course of human events, it becomes necessary for one people to dissolve the political bands which have connected them with another, and to assume among the powers of the earth, the separate and equal station to which the Laws of Nature and of Nature's God entitle them, a decent respect to the opinions of mankind requires that they should declare the causes which impel them to separation.—We hold these truths to be self-evident, that all men are created equal, that they are endowed by their Creator with certain unalienable Rights, that among these are Life, Liberty, and the pursuit of Happiness.—That to secure these rights, Governments are instituted among Men, deriving their just powers from the consent of the governed,—That whenever any Form of Government becomes destructive of these ends, it is the Right of the People to alter or to abolish it, and to institute new Government, laying its foundation on such principles and organizing its powers in such form, as to them shall seem most likely to effect their Safety and Happiness. . . .

We, therefore, the Representatives of the united States of America, in General Congress, Assembled, appealing to the Supreme Judge of the world for the rectitude of our intentions, do, in the Name and by the Authority of the good People of these Colonies, solemnly publish and declare, That these United Colonies are, and of Right ought to be Free and Independent States; that they are Absolved from all Allegiance to the British Crown, and that all political connection between them and the State of Great Britain, is and ought to be totally dissolved; and that as Free and Independent States, they have full Power to levy War, conclude Peace, contract Alliances, establish Commerce, and to do all other Acts and Things which Independent States may of right do.—And for the support of this Declaration, with a firm reliance on the protection of Divine Providence, we mutually pledge to each other our Lives, our Fortunes, and our sacred Honor.

PREAMBLE TO THE CONSTITUTION
OF THE UNITED STATES OF AMERICA

1789

We the People of the United States, in Order to form a more perfect Union, establish Justice, insure domestic Tranquility, provide for the common defence, promote the general Welfare, and secure the Blessings of Liberty to ourselves and our Posterity, do ordain and establish this CONSTITUTION for the United States of America.

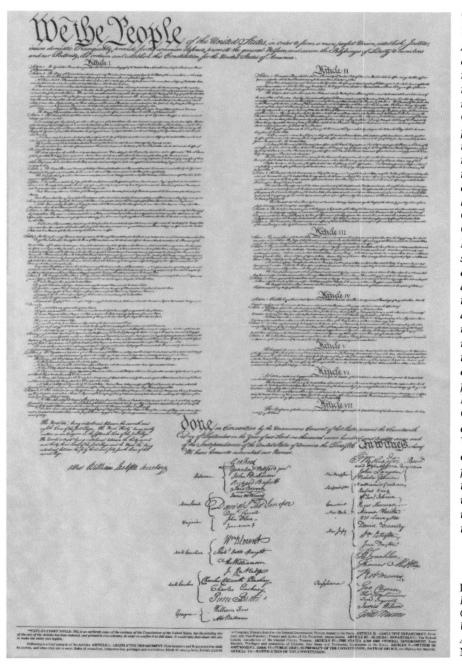

The constitution of the United States of America has been in continual use longer than any other country's governing document. The U.S. Constitution was first framed in Philadelphia in 1787 by a convention of delegates from twelve of the thirteen original colonies. The leader of the Convention was George Washington. By September of that same year, the first draft was completed and submitted to the thirteen states for approval. The vote of nine states was required for ratification, and the ninth vote came on June 21, 1788, from the state of New Hampshire. The Constitution became effective on the first Wednesday in March of 1789, guaranteeing from that day forward that the independence won from great Britain would be secured by the rule of law.

LEFT:
REPLICA OF THE CONSTITUTION OF THE UNITED STATES OF AMERICA, PAGE ONE
NATIONAL ARCHIVES

The Independence Day oration was an established American tradition in the mid-1800s. Townspeople would gather each Fourth of July to hear the nation's best speakers extol the virtues of their homeland. But on July 4, 1852, the citizens of Rochester, New York, heard a new kind of oration, and a new take on the subject of independence. Former slave Frederick Douglass, speaking that day to an audience ready for words of pride and praise, instead reminded the people of Rochester that their cherished independence meant little if it did not embrace Americans of all races. Born in 1817 on a Maryland plantation, Douglass learned to read—unusual and illegal for an American slave—at the age of eight through the tutoring of a woman in whose home he served as a house slave. At the age of twenty-one, Douglass escaped to New York City and began a career of speaking, writing, and traveling—all with one goal: freedom and independence for all Americans. Douglass was working as the editor of an abolition newspaper in Rochester when asked to give the Fourth of July address. The words he spoke surprised many but gave pause to all who treasured their freedom and truly believed in the American ideal of independence.

from an INDEPENDENCE DAY SPEECH AT ROCHESTER

Frederick Douglass, 1852

What, then, remains to be argued? Is it that slavery is not divine; that God did not establish it; that our doctors of divinity are mistaken? There is blasphemy in the thought. That which is inhuman cannot be divine! Who can reason on such a proposition? They that can may; I cannot. The time for such argument is past.

At a time like this, scorching iron, not convincing argument, is needed. O! had I the ability, and could I reach the nation's ear, I would today pour out a fiery stream of biting ridicule, blasting reproach, withering sarcasm, and stern rebuke. For it is not light that is needed, but fire; it is not the gentle shower, but thunder. We need the storm, the whirlwind, and the earthquake. The feeling of the nation must be quickened; the conscience of the nation must be roused; the propriety of the nation must be startled; the hypocrisy of the nation must be exposed; and its crimes against God and man must be proclaimed and denounced.

What, to the American slave, is your Fourth of July? I answer: a day that reveals to him, more than all other days in the year, the gross injustice and cruelty to which he is the constant victim. To him, your celebration is a shame; your boasted liberty, an unholy license; your national greatness, swelling vanity; your sounds of rejoicing are empty and heartless; your denunciation of tyrants, brass-fronted impudence; your shouts of liberty and equality, hollow mockery; your prayers and hymns, your sermons and thanksgivings, with all your religious parade and solemnity, are, to Him mere bombast, fraud, deception, impiety, and hypocrisy—a thin veil to cover up crimes which would disgrace a nation of savages. There is not a nation of savages, there is not a nation on the earth guilty of practices more shocking and bloody than are the people of the United States at this very hour.

Go where you may, search where you will, roam through all the monarchies and despotisms of the Old World, travel through South America, search out every abuse, and when you have found the last, lay your facts by the side of the everyday practices of this nation, and you will say with me that, for revolting barbarity and shameless hypocrisy, America reigns without a rival.

The first permanent English settlement in America was established by the London Company on Virginia's James River. Three ships landed on the banks of the James in 1606, carrying 104 male passengers who disembarked to found Jamestown. These brave, independent men fought great hardship and suffered terrible losses; but under the leadership of Captain John Smith, they held on, and the settlement survived.

ENGRAVING LEFT:
JAMESTOWN, 1606
LIBRARY OF CONGRESS

The second day of July, 1776, will be the most memorable epoch in the history of America. I am apt to believe that it will be celebrated by succeeding generations as the great anniversary festival. It ought to be commemorated as the day of deliverance, by solemn acts of devotion to God Almighty. It ought to be solemnized with pomp and parade, with shows, games, sports, guns, bells, bonfires, and illuminations, from one end of this continent to the other, from this time forward for evermore.

John Adams
A letter to Abigail Adams
July 3, 1776

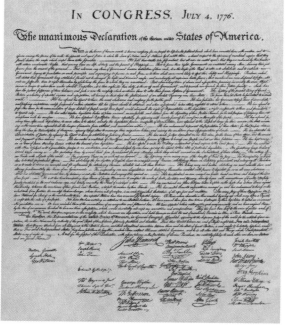

Is it so bad to be misunderstood? Pythagoras was misunderstood, and Socrates, and Jesus, and Luther, and Copernicus, and Galileo, and Newton, and every pure and wise spirit that ever took flesh. To be great is to be misunderstood.

Ralph Waldo Emerson
Self-Reliance

LEFT:
REPLICA OF DECLARATION OF INDEPENDENCE
NATIONAL ARCHIVES

Edwin Robert Peary reached the North Pole on April 6, 1909, along with his servant, Matt Hensen, and four eskimo guides. He was the first man to set foot on the world's northernmost point. Later that year, Dr. Frederick Cook claimed to have reached the Pole in April of 1908, a full year before Peary. The conflicting claims sparked a bitter debate that continued even after Congress recognized Peary's claim as first man on the Pole. Peary's achievement—braving the isolation and harshness of the Arctic climate—was a remarkable feat of independence, one that earned him a place among our nation's greatest explorers.

"TO THE BLACK HILLS, OR BUST"

The Gold Rush brought to the West a wave of independent souls seeking fortune and adventure. The Rush began in August 1848, when an article in the New York Herald *broke the news of the discovery of great deposits of gold in California. Later that year, President James K. Polk, in his annual message to Congress, fanned the flames with talk of the Gold Rush. In 1849 alone, 80,000 people made their way to California looking for the precious ore; their efforts were rewarded that year with finds worth a total of $10,000,000.*

THE SOLITUDE OF SELF

Elizabeth Cady Stanton, 1892

The strongest reason for giving woman all the opportunities for higher education, for the full development of her faculties, her forces of mind and body; for giving her the most enlarged freedom of thought and action; a complete emancipation from all forms of bondage, of custom, dependence, superstition; from all the crippling influences of fear—is the solitude and personal responsibility of her own individual life. The strongest reason why we ask for woman a voice in the government under which she lives; in the religion she is asked to believe; equality in social life, where she is the chief factor; a place in the trades and professions, where she may earn her bread, is because of her birthright to self-sovereignty; because, as an individual, she must rely on herself. No matter how much women prefer to lean, to be protected or supported, nor how much men desire to have them do so, they must make the voyage of life alone, and for safety in an emergency, they must know something of the laws of navigation. To guide our own craft, we must be captain, pilot, engineer; with chart and compass to stand at the wheel; to watch the winds and waves, and know when to take in the sail, and to read the signs in the firmament over all. It matters not whether the solitary voyager is man or woman; nature, having endowed them equally, leaves them to their own skill and judgment in the hour of danger, and, if not equal to the occasion, alike they perish.

To appreciate the importance of fitting every human soul for independent action, think for a moment of the immeasurable solitude of self. We come into the world alone, unlike all who have gone before us, we leave it alone, under circumstances peculiar to ourselves. No mortal ever has been, no mortal ever will be like the soul just launched on the sea of life. There can never again be just such a combination of prenatal influences; never again just such environments as make up the infancy, youth and manhood of this one. Nature never repeats herself, and the possibilities of one human soul will never be found in another. No one has ever found two blades of ribbon grass alike, and no one will ever find two human beings alike. Seeing, then, that what must be the infinite diversity in human character, we can in a measure appreciate the loss to a nation when any class of the people is uneducated and unrepresented in the government.

Elizabeth Cady Stanton was the leading American feminist of the nineteenth century. She organized the first American woman's rights convention at Seneca Falls, New York, in 1848. There, she for the first time publicly demanded the vote for American women. In her autobiography, Stanton recalls that when her only brother died and she heard her father lament that she had not been born a boy, she, at age ten, resolved to be as independent and self-reliant as boys were expected to be. She more than lived up to that promise; through her speaking and writing, Elizabeth Cady Stanton advanced the cause of true independence for American women more than any other individual of her generation. "The Solitude of Self," a speech delivered when Stanton was seventy-six years old, is still considered a classic for independent women. In this speech and in all that she did, Stanton did not ask the American public to give special consideration to women, but rather to afford to all citizens the rights and respect they deserved as human individuals and that they required in order to live productive, self-sufficient lives.

Amelia Earhart, born five years before the death of Elizabeth Cady Stanton, took up the former's cause of words with action, living the life of an independent, self-reliant woman. Earhart took her first flight in an airplane at the age of twenty-three; within two years, she was flying solo. In the next two decades Earhart recorded an impressive string of firsts: first woman to cross the Atlantic by air, first woman to cross the Atlantic by air alone, first woman to fly from Hawaii to the mainland U.S. alone, and in 1937, first to attempt a round-the-world air flight. This mission, never completed, was to be her last. Earhart's plane went down in the Pacific and was never recovered. She died as she would have wished, in flight, breaking new boundaries for American women.

from WALDEN

Henry David Thoreau, 1854

The mass of men lead lives of quiet desperation. What is called resignation is confirmed desperation. From the desperate city you go into the desperate country, and have to console yourself with the bravery of minks and muskrats. . . .

I went to the woods because I wished to live deliberately, to front only the essential facts of life, and see if I could not learn what it had to teach, and not, when I came to die, discover that I had not lived. I did not wish to live what was not life, living is so dear; nor did I wish to practise resignation, unless it was quite necessary. I wanted to live deep and suck out all the marrow of life, to live so sturdily and Spartan-like as to put to rest all that was not life, to cut a broad swath and shave close, to drive life into a corner, and reduce it to its lowest terms, and, if it proved to be mean, why then to get the whole and genuine meanness of it, and publish its meanness to the world. . . .

Time is but the stream I go a-fishing in. I drink at it; but while I drink I see the sandy bottom and detect how shallow it is.

Walden, *published in 1854, grew out of the two years Henry David Thoreau spent at Walden Pond in Massachusetts. Living simply and quietly in the woods, Thoreau hoped to strip his life down to its bare essentials and discover the truth impossible to find in the rush of nineteenth-century life. A true American individual, Thoreau believed that man must follow intuition over intellect. In his lifetime he made a name for himself through his essays and his ardent support of abolition. His* Civil Disobedience *has been an inspiration to such great leaders as Mahatma Ghandi and Martin Luther King, both of whom practiced Thoreau's concept of passive resistance in the face of oppressive authority. Few took notice of* Walden *upon its initial publication; but in the years since, it has become a worldwide classic, and its author has become an inspiration to all Americans with a streak of individuality.*

PAINTING RIGHT:
ADIRONDACK GUIDE, 1894
WINSLOW HOMER (1836-1910)

from SELF-RELIANCE

Ralph Waldo Emerson, 1841

Whoso would be a man, must be a nonconformist. He who would gather immortal palms must not be hindered by the name of goodness, but must explore if it be goodness. Nothing is at last sacred but the integrity of your own mind. Absolve you to yourself, and you shall have the suffrage of the world. I remember an answer which when quite young I was prompted to make to a valued adviser who was wont to importune me with the dear old doctrines of the church. On my saying, "What have I to do with the sacredness of traditions, if I live wholly from within?" my friend suggested,—"But these impulses may be from below, not from above." I replied, "They do not seem to me to be such; but if I am the Devil's child, I will live then from the Devil." No law can be sacred to me but that of my nature. Good and bad are but names very readily transferable to that or this; the only right is what is after my constitution; the only wrong is what is against it. A man is to carry himself in the presence of all opposition as if every thing were titular and ephemeral but he.

PAINTING ABOVE: [1961.281]
JUST A LITTLE SUNSHINE, C.1898
CHARLES MARION RUSSELL (1864-1926)
WATERCOLOR AND GRAPHITE ON PAPER
13⅛ X 9⅞ INCHES
AMON CARTER MUSEUM
FORT WORTH, TEXAS

The name Ralph Waldo Emerson is synonymous with the American independent spirit. In his writings, Emerson urged Americans to break free from the constraints of public opinion, of European tradition, and from anything at all that stifled their individual spirits. Through the years, the same independent spirit has run through various facets of American life. These cowboys in the American West—thousands of miles removed from the New England of Ralph Waldo Emerson—embody the same free-thinking, solitary way of life advocated in Self-Reliance.

PAINTING RIGHT: [1961.282]
JUST A LITTLE RAIN, C.1898
CHARLES M. RUSSELL (1864-1926)
WATERCOLOR AND GRAPHITE ON PAPER
12¾ X 11⅞ INCHES
AMON CARTER MUSEUM
FORT WORTH, TEXAS

THE PASSION FOR EXPLORATION

Bring me men to match my mountains,
Bring me men to match my plains;
Men with empires in their purpose,
And new eras in their brains.
Bring me men to match my prairies,
Men to match my inland seas;
Men whose thoughts shall prove a highway
Up to ample destinies;
Bring me men to match my mountains—
Bring me men.

Sam W. Foss
from "The Coming American"

PAINTING ABOVE: [1967.27]
VIEW OF PIKE'S PEAK, 1872
GEORGE CALEB BINGHAM (1811-1879)
OIL ON CANVAS
28 x 42⅛ INCHES
AMON CARTER MUSEUM
FORT WORTH, TEXAS

Born in 1830 in Germany, Albert Bierstadt emigrated with his parents in 1831 to New Bedford, Massachusetts. He returned to Germany at the age of twenty-three to study art, but throughout his career, the American landscape would be his subject. After a few years of painting in New Hampshire's White Mountains, Bierstadt was enticed by a spirit of exploration to go west. There he found the spectacular mountain scenes that would become the inspiration for his greatest paintings. In the 1860s and 1870s, Bierstadt was considered among the best of American painters. Later in his lifetime, his grandiose style of landscape painting fell out of favor, and his work was disregarded by collectors and critics. Today, however, the paintings of Albert Bierstadt are treasured by Americans for their dramatic style and their documentation of the discovery of the West.

MEN TO MATCH MY MOUNTAINS

from "The Coming American"
Sam W. Foss

Bring me men to match my mountains,
Bring me men to match my plains;
Men with empires in their purpose,
And new eras in their brains.
Bring me men to match my prairies,
Men to match my inland seas;
Men whose thoughts shall prove a highway
Up to ample destinies;
Bring me men to match my mountains—
Bring me men.

Bring me men to match my forests,
Strong to fight the storm and blast,
Branching toward the skyey future
Rooted in the fertile past;
Bring me men to match my valleys,
Tolerant of sun and snow,
Men out of whose faithful purpose
Time's consummate blooms shall grow;
Men to tame the tigerish instincts
Of the lair, the cave, and den,
Cleanse the dragon, slime of nature—
Bring me men.

Bring me men to match my rivers,
Continent cleavers, flowing free;
Men of oceanic impulse,
Men whose moral currents sweep
Toward the wide-infolding ocean
Of the undiscovered deep;
Men who feel the strong pulsation
Of the central sea, and then
Time their current to its throb—
Bring me men.

PAINTING ABOVE: [1966.1]
SUNRISE, YOSEMITE VALLEY, C. 1870
ALBERT BIERSTADT (1830-1902)
OIL ON CANVAS
36½ X 52⅜ INCHES
AMON CARTER MUSEUM
FORT WORTH, TEXAS

THE LEWIS AND CLARK EXPEDITION
from the diary of Meriwether Lewis, 1805

ARIEL

Here the mountainous country again approaches the river on the left, and a higher mountain is distinguished towards the southwest. At a distance of twenty miles from our camp we halted at a village of Wahkiacums. . . . We merely stopped to purchase some food and two beaver skins, and then proceeded. Opposite to these islands the hills on the left retire, and the river widens into a kind of bay crowded with low islands, subject to be overflowed occasionally by the tide. We had not gone far from this village when the fog cleared off, and we enjoyed the delightful prospect of the ocean; that ocean, the object of all our labours, the reward of all our anxieties. This cheering view exhilarated the spirits of all the party, who were still more delighted on hearing the distant roar of the breakers. We went on with great cheerfulness under the high mountainous country which continued along the right bank; the shore was however so bold and rocky, that we could not, until after going fourteen miles from the last village, find any spot fit for an encampment. At that distance, having made during the day thirty-four miles, we spread our mats on the ground, and passed the night.

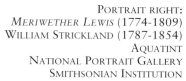

PORTRAIT RIGHT:
MERIWETHER LEWIS (1774-1809)
WILLIAM STRICKLAND (1787-1854)
AQUATINT
NATIONAL PORTRAIT GALLERY
SMITHSONIAN INSTITUTION

In 1804 President Thomas Jefferson commissioned Meriwether Lewis and William Clark to explore the land from the Mississippi River to the Pacific Ocean which had been acquired in the Louisiana Purchase. Their party left St. Louis on May 14, 1804, and arrived on the shores of the Pacific on November 8, 1805. In the words of President Theodore Roosevelt, Lewis and Clark "opened the door into the heart of the far West" and began the great westward expansion of America.

PAINTING LEFT: [1961.195]
LEWIS AND CLARK ON THE LOWER COLUMBIA, 190
CHARLES MARION RUSSELL (1864-1926)
GOUACHE, WATERCOLOR, AND GRAPHITE ON PAPER
18¾ x 23⅞ INCHES
AMON CARTER MUSEUM
FORT WORTH, TEXAS

from MEMOIRS OF MY LIFE

John Charles Frémont

The Bay . . . is separated from the sea by low mountain ranges. Looking from the peaks of the Sierra Nevada, the coast mountains present an apparently continuous line, with only a single gap. . . . This is the entrance to the great bay, and is the only water communication from the coast to the interior country. On the south, the bordering mountains come down in a narrow ridge of broken hills . . . against which the sea breaks heavily. On the northern side, the mountain presents a bold promontory, rising in a few miles to a height of two or three thousand feet. Between these points is the strait—about one mile broad in the narrowest part, and five miles long from the sea to the bay. To the Gate I gave the name of *Chrysopylae*, or Golden Gate; for the same reasons that the harbor of Byzantium (Constantinople afterwards), was called *Chrysoceras*, or Golden Horn. Directly fronting the entrance, mountains a few miles from the shore rise about two thousand feet above the water, crowned by a forest of lofty cypress. . . . Behind, the rugged peak of Mount Diavolo, nearly four thousand feet high, overlooks the surrounding country. . . . It presents a varied character of rugged and broken hills, rolling and undulating land, and rich alluvial shores backed by fertile and wooded ranges, suitable for towns, villages, and farms, with which it is beginning to be dotted.

John Charles Frémont made his first expedition in 1842, exploring the route from the Mississippi River to Oregon by way of the Continental Divide. On this and later trips, Frémont compiled detailed maps of the western landscape that were used by scientists and by emigrants looking for the safest and most passable routes to the West. By 1856 Frémont had achieved such fame and popularity with the American public that the Republican party chose him as their candidate in the presidential election.

PORTRAIT RIGHT:
JOHN CHARLES FRÉMONT (1813-1890)
WILLIAM S. JEWETT (1812-1873)
OIL ON PANEL
NATIONAL PORTRAIT GALLERY
SMITHSONIAN INSTITUTION

Wagon trains made slow, hard progress across rough terrain, carrying the greatest American explorers—the families of pioneers who populated the western half of our nation. The first organized wagon train to California was planned in February of 1841 and launched later that spring. In all, fifteen wagons carrying sixty-nine people set out from Missouri for the nearly six-month journey across the Rocky Mountains to the Pacific Coast. In the years that followed, wagon trains heading west would increase in size to more than 120 wagons—all part of the Great Emigration that continued until 1869 when the newly completed transcontinental railroad gave emigrants a faster, more comfortable ride to the West.

from PIONEERS! O PIONEERS!

Walt Whitman, 1865 (revision, 1881)

O you youths, Western youths,
So impatient, full of action, full of manly pride and friendship,
Plain I see you Western youths, see you tramping with the foremost,
Pioneers! O pioneers!

Have the elder races halted?
Do they droop and end their lesson, wearied over there beyond the seas?
We take up the task eternal, and the burden and the lesson,
Pioneers! O pioneers!

All the past we leave behind,
We debouch upon a newer mightier world, varied world,
Fresh and strong the world we seize, world of labor and the march,
    Pioneers! O pioneers!

    Colorado men are we,
From the peaks gigantic, from the great sierras and the high plateaus,
From the mine and from the gully, from the hunting trail we come,
    Pioneers! O pioneers!

    From Nebraska, from Arkansas,
Central inland race are we, from Missouri, with continental blood intervein'd,
All the hands of comrades clasping, all the Southern, all the Northern,
    Pioneers! O pioneers!

THE OREGON TRAIL

Mary Patton Taylor, as told to Sara B. Wrenn, 1939

When my folks got to Oregon they settled in the Waldo Hills. They settled on their claim just three days after they arrived. My grandparents got here in September, and in November father and mother was married. The only thing mother had to start housekeeping with was a plate. She paid fifty cents for it, and she earned the fifty cents sewing three days for a woman in the Waldo Hills. Father wasn't much better off than mother. He wasn't twenty-one years old, and so he couldn't take a claim. And he didn't have any money, because all he made crossing the plains was his food and bed and fifteen dollars that he got for driving grandfather's oxen. But he wanted to get married, and, when he got there, he went to work for a man named Nicholas Shrum right away. He split rails for Shrum, and all he got was thirty-seven-and-a-half cents a hundred. Can you beat that? Just as soon as father had $2.25 he thought, Maybe that's enough to pay the preacher. When father and mother was married, father paid over the $2.25. He must have looked kind of poor about it, for right away Elder Simpson asked him how much money he had left, and father said that was all, and then Elder Simpson handed it back to him, telling him he needed it most. But father was gritty. He said, "If my girl's worth marrying, I'm willing to spend all I have to get her." And he made Elder Simpson keep the $2.25.

Painting above:
The Oregon Trail, 1869
Albert Bierstadt (1830-1902)
The Butler Institute of American Art
Youngstown, Ohio

The wagons which were home to American pioneers for six months at a time while they crossed the plains and the mountains on their way to the West were far from luxurious. Constructed of wood and some iron, they rode on rough wooden wheels and had no springs to soften the ride. The wagon beds were simple rectangular boxes, at most twelve feet long; protection from the elements came in the form of canvas stretched across hickory bows. The families rose at dawn to make breakfast and prepare for a full day of slow, painstaking travel. With such hardships en route, all the pioneers—men, women, and children alike—required great endurance in order to see the trip to its finish.

DOWN THE SANTA FE TRAIL

from the diary of Susan Shelby Magoffin, 1846

It was now after 9 o'clock and quite damp. So just as soon as our tent could be stretched and the bed made, which took us till after 10—I slipped off to roost. I was so tired I could not sleep; it commenced raining too and beat so near my head, I thought every minute I must surely get a ducking, but I kept dry though, and a little before daylight got a short nap.

Soon the wagoners were stirring, anxious to cross the creek before it should rain any more. The principal passway was blocked by Col. Owens' wagons, so they doubled teams and cut around to make one of their own. The tent was soon knocked up and off we came to "Cotton Wood" to get our breakfast, for we had not a stick of wood to cook with there, and hungry necessity compelled us to come, we had had nothing to eat since dinner yesterday. We crossed the creek without difficulty, the banks are long but not very steep; the rain has made them quite slippy, but our little light carriages passed them easy. We got our dinner, or rather breakfast about 1 o'clock. Seven of the wagons with doubled teams came over this morning, the others are coming in now, late p.m.

If any young man is about to commence in the world, with little in his circumstances to prepossess him in favor of one section above another, we say to him publicly and privately: Go to the West; there your capacities are sure to be appreciated and your industry and energy rewarded.

Horace Greeley

PAINTING ABOVE:
AMONG THE SIERRA NEVADA MOUNTAINS, 1868
ALBERT BIERSTADT (1830-1902)
OIL ON CANVAS
NATIONAL MUSEUM OF AMERICAN ART
SMITHSONIAN INSTITUTION

As [my sister] with the other friends turned to leave me for the ferry which was to take them back to home and civilization, I stood alone on that wild prairie. . . .

Looking westward, I saw my husband driving slowly over the plain; turning my face once more to the East, my dear sister's footsteps were fast widening the distance between us. For the time I knew not which way to go, nor whom to follow, but in a few moments I rallied my forces. . . . and soon overtook the slowly moving oxen who were bearing my husband and child over the green prairie.

Lavinia Porter
from a journal of life on the Oregon Trail

PRINT LEFT:
LIFE ON A WAGON TRAIN
LIBRARY OF CONGRESS

Now is the time to take longer strides—time for a great new enterprise—time for this nation to take a clearly leading role in space achievements which, in many ways, may hold the key to our future on earth. . . . I believe that this nation should commit itself to achieving the goal, before this decade is out, of landing a man on the moon and returning him safely to earth. No single space project in this period will be more impressive to mankind or more important for the long-range exploration of space. And none will be so difficult to accomplish. . . . Let it be clear that this is a judgment which the members of the Congress must finally make. Let it be clear that I am asking the Congress and the country to accept a firm commitment to a new course of action. . . . I believe we should go to the moon. . . .

President John Fitzgerald Kennedy
Speech to Congress, May 25, 1961

PORTRAIT LEFT:
JOHN MUIR (1838-1914)
ORLANDO ROULAND (1871-1945)
OIL ON CANVAS
NATIONAL PORTRAIT GALLERY
SMITHSONIAN INSTITUTION

Modern-day American explorers owe a debt of gratitude to John Muir, the Scottish-born American explorer, naturalist, conservationist, and writer. Muir was thirty years old when he first laid eyes upon the Sierra Nevada Mountains in California; from that point on, he devoted his life to exploring and writing about these magnificent mountains and advocating the cause of conservation in Washington. With the help of Muir, two of our most beloved national parks—Sequoia and Yosemite—were founded in 1890. Two years later, Muir founded the Sierra Club, which to this day carries on his legacy of exploration, appreciation, and conservation of our natural resources.

THE MOUNTAINS OF CALIFORNIA

John Muir, 1894

The walls of these park valleys of the Yosemite kind are made up of rocks mountains in size, partly separated from each other by narrow gorges and side-cañons; and they are so sheer in front, and so compactly built together on a level floor, that, comprehensively seen, the parks they inclose look like immense halls or temples lighted from above. Every rock seems to glow with life. Some lean back in majestic repose; others, absolutely sheer, or nearly so, for thousands of feet, advance their brows in thoughtful attitudes beyond their companions, giving welcome to storms and calms alike, seemingly conscious yet heedless of everything going on about them, awful in stern majesty, types of permanence, yet associated with beauty of the frailest and most fleeting forms; their feet set in pine-groves and gay emerald meadows, their brows in the sky; bathed in light, bathed in floods of singing water, while snow-clouds, avalanches, and the winds shine and surge and wreathe about them as the years go by, as if into these mountain mansions Nature had taken pains to gather their choicest treasures to draw her lovers into close and confiding communion with her.

PAINTING RIGHT:
[47.1268]
THE BUFFALO TRAIL, 1867-1868
ALBERT BIERSTADT (1830-1902)
OIL ON CANVAS
32 X 48 INCHES
GIFT OF MRS. MAXIM KAROLIK FOR THE M. AND M. KAROLIK COLLECTION OF AMERICAN PAINTINGS 1815-1865
MUSEUM OF FINE ARTS
BOSTON, MASSACHUSETTS

Early explorers of the American West found the bison—or buffalo—in abundance. Estimates are that in the early nineteenth century, more than sixty million bison roamed the North American plains. By 1873, however, the bison was nearly extinct in America, with fewer than one thousand remaining, due in large part to professional hunters who shot their game from the windows of railroad cars. The extermination of the bison was stopped before they disappeared entirely, however, and Americans learned a valuable lesson about their country's natural resources and the need to protect and preserve them. Today, we cherish the bison as one of the enduring symbols of the American West.

AMERICA THE BEAUTIFUL
Katharine Lee Bates, 1893

O beautiful for spacious skies,
For amber waves of grain,
For purple mountain majesties
Above the fruited plain!
America! America!
God shed His grace on thee
And crown thy good with brotherhood
From sea to shining sea!

O beautiful for pilgrim feet,
Whose stern, impassioned stress
A thoroughfare for freedom beat
Across the wilderness!
America! America!
God mend thine every flaw,
Confirm thy soul in self-control,
Thy liberty in law!

O beautiful for heroes proved
In liberating strife,
Who more than self their country loved,
And mercy more than life!

America! America!
May God thy gold refine,
Till all success be nobleness
And every gain divine!

O beautiful for patriot dream
That sees beyond the years
Thine alabaster cities gleam
Undimmed by human tears!

America! America!
God shed His grace on thee,
And crown thy good with brotherhood
From sea to shining sea!

Painting left: [1972.45]
Scene on the Columbia River,
c. 1852
John Mix Stanley (1814-1872)
Oil on canvas
17⅛ x 21⅛ inches
Amon Carter Museum
Fort Worth, Texas

American explorers have come in every form—from the brave first settlers who crossed a great ocean to face a complete unknown to the pioneers who left their homes and families behind to seek a better life in the West. From the trappers and businessmen to the poets and missionaries, all have shared a similar spirit of adventure and curiosity. Katharine Lee Bates, an English professor at Wellesley College in Massachusetts, was touring the West in the summer of 1893 when she wrote the words that would become "America the Beautiful." Her poem—an expression of an Easterner's awe at the grandeur of the mountainous West and at the unlimited possibilities for the American future—has become a symbol of the pride every American feels when he or she ponders the great promise of our nation.

A CITADEL
OF CONFIDENCE

Oh it's home again, America for me!
Our hearts are turning home again
and there we long to be,
In our beautiful big country
beyond the ocean bars,
Where the air is full of sunlight
and the flag is full of stars.

Now it's home again, and home again,
our hearts are turning west,
Of all the lands beneath the sun
America is best.
We're going home to our own folks,
beyond the ocean bars,
Where the air is full of sunlight
and the flag is full of stars.

Henry Van Dyke
from "America's Welcome Home"

PAINTING RIGHT:
YOSEMITE LANDSCAPE
ALBERT BIERSTADT (1830-1902)

from HISTORY OF PLYMOUTH PLANTATION

William Bradford, 1620

But hear I cannot but stay and make a pause, and stand half amased at this poore peoples presente condition; and so I thinke will the reader too, when he well considers the same. Being thus passed the vast ocean, and a sea of troubles before in their preparation . . . they had now no freinds to wellcome them, nor inns to entertaine or refresh their weatherbeaten bodys, no houses or much less townes to repaire to, to seeke for succoure. . . . And for the season it was winter, and they that know the winters of that cuntrie know them to be sharp and violent, and subjecte to cruell and feirce stormes, deangerous to travill to known places, much more to serch an unknown coast. Besides, what could they see but a hidious and desolate wildernes, full of wild beasts and willd men? and what multituds of them ther might be of them they knew not. Nether could they, as it were, goe up to the tope of Pisgah, to vew from the willdernes a more goodly cuntrie to feed their hops; for which way soever they turnd their eys (save upward to the heavens) they could have litle solace or content in respecte of any outward objects. For summer being done, all things stand upon them with a wetherbeaten face; and the whole countrie, full of woods and thickets, represented a wild and savage heiw. . . .

What could now sustaine them but the spirite of God and his grace? May not and ought not the children of these fathers rightly say: *Our faithers were Englishmen which came over this great ocean, and were ready to perish in the willdernes; but they cried unto the Lord, and he heard their voyce, and looked on their adversitie, etc. Let them therfore praise the Lord, because he is good, and his mercies endure for ever. Yea, let them which have been redeemed of the Lord, shew how he hath delivered them from the hand of the oppressour. When they wandered in the deserte willdernes out of the way, and found no citie to dwell in, both hungrie, and thirstie, their sowle was overwhelmed in them. Let them confess before the Lord his loving kindnes, and his wonderfull works before the sons of men.* . . .

William Bradford wrote his history of Plymouth Plantation to document the colony's history and to restate its mission to found a new, purer church in the New World. Today, we also value Bradford's writings as a testament to the confidence and faith of the Pilgrims who, despite great odds against them, believed that they could settle and thrive in America. We owe the very foundation of our nation to the confidence and perseverance of these and other seventeenth-century settlers; for once they had settled and begun to thrive on American soil—although British colonies by law—they had begun to form the American nation. The signers of the Declaration of Independence looked back upon William Bradford and his contemporaries much as we look back upon historical figures like Thomas Jefferson and George Washington—to understand our common heritage and to take inspiration from the courage and confidence of Americans who have made the country what it is today.

THE BIRTH OF A NATION

John Adams
from a letter to his wife,
Abigail Adams, July 3, 1776

Yesterday, the greatest question was decided, which ever was debated in America, and a greater, perhaps, never was nor will be decided among men. A resolution was passed without one dissenting colony, "that these United Colonies are, and of right ought to be, free and independent States, and as such they have, and of right ought to have, full power to make war, conclude peace, establish commerce, and to do all other acts and things which other States may rightfully do." You will see in a few days a Declaration setting forth the causes which have impelled us to this mighty revolution, and the reasons which will justify it in the sight of God and man. A plan of confederation will be taken up in a few days.

You will think me transported with enthusiasm, but I am not. I am well aware of the toil, and blood, and treasure, that it will cost us to maintain this declaration, and support and defend these States. Yet, through all the gloom, I can see the rays of ravishing light and glory. I can see that the end is more than worth all the means, and that posterity will triumph in that day's transaction, even although we should rue it, which I trust in God we shall not.

General Lee was leading his Confederate troops toward Washington, D.C., from the west in the summer of 1863 when he met Union forces at Gettysburg, Pennsylvania. From the first of July through the third, the Battle of Gettysburg raged, ending as the bloodiest in the Civil War: the North counted 23,000 casualties, the South 30,000. It was just over four months later, on November 19, that President Lincoln traveled to Gettysburg to deliver his address at the dedication of a national cemetery on the battle site. The above photo shows Lincoln in the crowd at Gettysburg. His address, only three short paragraphs in length, was a solemn tribute to the fallen soldiers on both sides but also a confident recommitment to the cause—not that of the North or of the South—but of preserving the United States of America.

THE GETTYSBURG ADDRESS

Abraham Lincoln, 1863

Four score and seven years ago our fathers brought forth on this continent, a new nation, conceived in Liberty, and dedicated to the proposition that all men are created equal.

Now we are engaged in a great civil war, testing whether that nation, or any nation so conceived and so dedicated, can long endure. We are met on a great battlefield of that war. We have come to dedicate a portion of that field, as a final resting place for those who here gave their lives that that nation might live. It is altogether fitting and proper that we should do this.

But, in a larger sense, we can not dedicate—we can not consecrate—we can not hallow—this ground. The brave men, living and dead, who struggled here, have consecrated it, far above our poor power to add or detract. The world will little note, nor long remember what we say here, but it can never forget what they did here. It is for us the living, rather, to be dedicated here to the unfinished work which they who fought here have thus far so nobly advanced. It is rather for us to be here dedicated to the great task remaining before us—that from these honored dead we take increased devotion to that cause for which they gave the last full measure of devotion—that we here highly resolve that these dead shall not have died in vain—that this nation, under God, shall have a new birth of freedom— and that government of the people, by the people, for the people, shall not perish from the earth.

Abraham Lincoln spoke only a few short moments at Gettysburg in the autumn of 1863, but his words continue to echo in the hearts and minds of the American people well over one hundred years later. Memorized by schoolchildren, analyzed by historians, and quoted in an endless volume of books and papers, the Gettysburg Address may well be the most beloved three paragraphs in American history. The President's eloquent expression of the noble tragedy of the Civil War has a timeless appeal to all Americans who believe that their confidence and patriotism must be tempered by sensitivity and humility.

Immigrants flooded America's eastern shore in the late nineteenth century full of confidence and ready to begin new lives in a new world. Ellis Island, off New York City, was a receiving station for immigrants for more than sixty years. In that time nearly twenty million new Americans passed through its processing center on their way to the mainland United States. Today countless families trace their American roots to a confident individual whose first American experience was waiting in line at Ellis Island.

The American continents, by the free and independent condition which they have assumed and maintained, are henceforth not to be considered as subjects for future colonization by any European powers.

James Monroe

George M. Cohan was the living definition of the patriotic American—boldly confident that his country was the best place on earth. Cohan is remembered for many things—his singing, his composing, his Broadway shows—but perhaps most beloved for the song "Over There." Written in 1917, the song was a symbolic bugle call, urging all Americans to join the fight for freedom, and warning all the world to prepare for the confident, courageous American forces. During World War I, the song became an American anthem; Cohan was later recognized for his contribution to the national spirit during wartime with the Congressional Medal of Honor.

Johnnie get your gun, get your gun, get your gun,
Take it on the run, on the run, on the run;
Hear them calling you and me;
Ev'ry son of liberty.
Hurry right away, no delay, go today,
Make your daddy glad, to have had such a lad,
Tell your sweetheart not to pine,
To be proud her boy's in line.

Over there, over there,
Send the word, send the word over there,
That the Yanks are coming,
The Yanks are coming,
The drums rum-tumming ev'ry where—

So prepare, say a pray'r,
Send the word, send the word to beware,
We'll be over, we're coming over,
And we won't come back till it's over over there.

George M. Cohan
"Over There"

Soldiers, sailors, and airmen of the Allied expeditionary force: You are about to embark upon a great crusade toward which we have striven these many months. The eyes of the world are upon you. The hopes and prayers of liberty-loving peoples everywhere march with you. . . . Your task will not be an easy one. Your enemy is well trained, well equipped, and battle-hardened. He will fight savagely. But this is the year 1944. Much has happened since the Nazi triumphs of 1940–41. . . . The tide has turned. The free men of the world are marching together to victory.

General Dwight D. Eisenhower
D-Day Order of the Day
June 6, 1944

PHOTOGRAPH LEFT:
POLITICAL
MEMORABILIA

Let us compare every constitution we have seen with that of the United States of America, and we shall have no reason to blush for our country. On the contrary, we shall feel the strongest motives to fall upon our knees, in gratitude to heaven for having graciously pleased to give us birth and education in that country, and for having destined us to live under her laws!

John Adams

PHOTOGRAPH ABOVE:
SAILORS ON PARADE
ARCHIVE PHOTOS

THE STARS AND STRIPES FOREVER

John Philip Sousa, 1898

Let martial note in triumph float,
And liberty extend its mighty hand,
A flag appears,
'Mid thund'rous cheers,
The banner of the Western land.
The emblem of the brave and true,
Its folds protect no tyrant crew,
The red and white and starry blue,
Is Freedom's shield and hope.

Let the eagle shriek from lofty peak,
The never-ending watchword of our land.
Let summer breeze
Waft through the trees
The echo of the chorus grand.
Sing out for liberty and light,
Sing out for freedom and the right,
Sing out for Union and its might,
Oh, patriotic Sons!

Other nations may deem their flags the best
And cheer them with fervid elation,
But the flag of the North
And South and West
Is the flag of flags, the flag of
Freedom's nation.

Hurrah for the flag of the free,
May it wave as our standard forever,
The gem of the land and the sea,
The Banner of the Right.

Let despots remember the day
When our fathers with mighty endeavor,
Proclaim'd as they march'd to the fray,
That by their might, and by their right,
It waves forever!

John Philip Sousa was born in 1854. His father was a trombone player in the United States Marine Band. As an adult, Sousa followed his father's footsteps into the Marine Band, eventually becoming its leader. Forever connected in American minds with confident, unabashed patriotism, Sousa made many contributions to American life, but perhaps his most memorable is the stirring "The Stars and Stripes Forever." Sousa wrote the anthem on board a ship returning to America from an extended visit to Europe. He later said that as he stood on board thinking of home, he was struck by a vision of the flag: "I could see the stars and stripes flying from the flagstaff of the White House just as plainly as if I were back there again . . . and to my imagination, it seemed to be the biggest, grandest flag in the world." The words to the song, reprinted above, are not as familiar to all Americans as the notes of the march, but they share the same energy and patriotic spirit evoked by the music.

PORTRAIT RIGHT,
JOHN PHILIP SOUSA (1854-1932)
SEVENTEENTH DIRECTOR "THE PRESIDENT'S OWN"
OFFICIAL U.S. MARINE BAND PHOTO

Daniel Boone was one of the first heroes of the American frontier. In the mid-1700s, Boone explored the area that would become Kentucky and founded a settlement at Boonesborough. Boone also led the expedition that blazed the Wilderness Road through the Cumberland Gap from the Shenandoah Valley into Kentucky. This road became the major thoroughfare for pioneer settlers in the region, most of whom treasured the stories and legends of a man named Daniel Boone.

THE EMIGRANTS
John Greenleaf Whittier

We cross the prairie as of old
    The Pilgrims crossed the sea,
    To make the West, as they the East,
The homestead of the free.

We go to rear a wall of men
    On Freedom's southern line,
And plant beside the cotton tree
    The rugged Northern pine!

We're flowing from our native hills
    As our free rivers flow:
The blessing of our Mother-land
    Is on us as we go.

We go to plant her common schools
    On distant prairie swells,
And give the Sabbaths of the wild
    The music of her bells.

Upbearing, like the Ark of old,
    The Bible in our van,
We go to test the truth of God
    Against the fraud of man.

No pause, nor rest, save where the streams
    That feed the Kansas run,
Save where our Pilgrim gonfalon
    Shall flout the setting sun!

We'll tread the prairie as of old
    Our fathers sailed the sea,
And make the West, as they the East,
    The homestead of the free!

PAINTING LEFT:
DANIEL BOONE ESCORTING PIONEERS
GEORGE CALEB BINGHAM (1811-1879)

AMERICA'S WELCOME HOME

Henry Van Dyke

Oh, gallantly they fared forth in khaki and in blue,
America's crusading host of warriors bold and true;
They battled for the rights of men beside our brave Allies.
And now they're coming home to us with glory in their eyes.

Oh it's home again, America for me!
Our hearts are turning home again and there we long to be,
In our beautiful big country beyond the ocean bars,
Where the air is full of sunlight and the flag is full of stars.

They bore our country's great word across the rolling sea,
"America swears brotherhood with all the just and free."
They wrote that word victorious on fields of mortal strife,
And many a valiant lad was proud to seal it with his life.

Oh, welcome home in Heaven's peace, dear spirits of the dead!
And welcome home ye living sons America has bred!
The lords of war are beaten down, your glorious task is done;
You fought to make the whole world free, and the victory is won.

Now it's home again, and home again, our hearts are turning west,
Of all the lands beneath the sun America is best.
We're going home to our own folks, beyond the ocean bars,
Where the air is full of sunlight and the flag is full of stars.

PHOTOGRAPH LEFT:
YOUNG PATRIOT,
WORLD WAR I
FPG INTERNATIONAL

Americans have never entered into battle lightly, but when peace and freedom have been threatened at home or abroad, we have always risen confidently to the challenge, ready to fight and to sacrifice. But wars are not won only on the battlefield; soldiers in the field need the confidence and the support of those at home to carry them through. In our art and our literature, we express our support of and gratitude for those who put their lives on the line for their country and for the good of all mankind.

PAINTING ABOVE:
ALLIES DAY, MAY 1917
CHILDE F. HASSAM (1859-1935)
NATIONAL GALLERY OF ART,
WASHINGTON, D.C.

THE FOUR FREEDOMS

Franklin Delano Roosevelt, 1941

In the future days, which we seek to make secure, we look forward to a world founded upon four essential human freedoms.

The first is freedom of speech and expression—everywhere in the world.

The second is freedom of every person to worship God in his own way—everywhere in the world.

The third is freedom from want—which, translated into world terms, means economic understandings which will secure to every nation a healthy peacetime life for its inhabitants—everywhere in the world.

The fourth is freedom from fear—which, translated into world terms, means a worldwide reduction of armaments to such a point and in such a thorough fashion that no nation will be in a position to commit an act of physical aggression against any neighbor—anywhere in the world.

That is no vision of a distant millennium. It is a definite basis for a kind of world attainable in our own time and generation. That kind of world is the very antithesis of the so-called new order of tyranny which the dictators seek to create with the crash of a bomb.

I WANT YOU F.D.R. STAY AND FINISH THE JOB!

INDEPENDENT VOTERS' COMMITTEE OF THE ARTS *and* SCIENCES *for* ROOSEVELT

POSTER LEFT:
FRANKLIN DELANO ROOSEVELT
THIRTY-SECOND PRESIDENT OF THE
UNITED STATES
JAMES MONTGOMERY FLAGG
(1877-1960)
COLOR HALFTONE POSTER
NATIONAL PORTRAIT GALLERY
SMITHSONIAN INSTITUTION

Elected to the presidency four times, Franklin Delano Roosevelt served from 1933 to 1945 and led the American people through the Great Depression and the Second World War. When he took office in 1933, however, Roosevelt's greatest challenge was neither the economy nor national defense but the sagging confidence of the people. With his stirring speeches and comforting Fireside Chats, FDR portrayed an image of a leader in full command of his office and renewed the faith of Americans in their government and in themselves, preparing them to meet the great challenges of the day.

THE ONLY THING WE HAVE TO FEAR IS FEAR ITSELF
Franklin Delano Roosevelt, 1933

This is preeminently the time to speak the truth, the whole truth, frankly and boldly. Nor need we shrink from honestly facing conditions in our country today. This great Nation will endure as it has endured, will revive and will prosper. So, first of all, let me assert my firm belief that the only thing we have to fear is fear itself—nameless, unreasoning, unjustified terror which paralyzes needed efforts to convert retreat into advance. In every dark hour of our national life a leadership of frankness and vigor has met with that understanding and support of the people themselves which is essential to victory. I am convinced that you will again give the support to leadership in these critical days.

PAINTING ABOVE:
FARM LANDSCAPE
GRANT WOOD (1892-1942)

A TRADITION
OF FAITH

Almighty God, Who has given us
this good land for our heritage, . . .
Bless our land with honorable industry,
sound learning, and pure manners.
Save us from violence, discord
and confusion, from pride and arrogance,
and from every evil way.
Defend our liberties, and fashion into
one united people the multitude
brought hither out of many
kindreds and tongues.

Thomas Jefferson
from "A National Prayer"

The faith of our first Puritan settlers laid the foundation for our nation. The Puritans—led by John Winthrop—settled Massachusetts Bay Colony in the belief that they were God's chosen people, entrusted with the task of founding a pure outpost of the church in the wilderness of the New World. It was their unshakable faith that saw them through the difficult early years of life in New England. John and Priscilla Alden, pictured at right, were residents of the Plymouth Colony, located to the south of the Puritan settlements. The men and women who settled Plymouth—known as the Pilgrims—were driven to the New World by their desire to freely practice their religion, and they, too, helped establish faith as one of the guiding principles of American life.

A MODELL OF CHRISTIAN CHARITY

John Winthrop, 1630

Thus stands the cause betweene God and us, we are entered into Covenant with him for this worke, wee have taken out a Commission. . . . the Lord will be our God and delight to dwell among us, as his owne people and will commaund a blessing upon us in all our wayes, soe that wee shall see much more of his wisdome power goodnes and truthe then formerly wee have beene acquainted with, wee shall finde that the God of Israell is among us, when tenn of us shall be able to resist a thousand of our enemies, when hee shall make us a prayse and glory, that men shall say of succeeding plantacions: the lord make it like that of New England: for wee must Consider that wee shall be as a Citty upon a Hill, the eies of all people are uppon us; soe that if wee shall deale falsely with our god in this worke wee have undertaken and soe cause him to withdrawe his present help from us, wee shall be made a story and a by-word through the world, wee shall open the mouthes of enemies to speake evill of the wayes of god and all professours for Gods sake; wee shall shame the faces of many of gods worthy servants, and cause theire prayers to be turned into Cursses upon us till wee be consumed out of the good land whether wee are goeing: . . .wee are Commaunded this day to love the Lord our God, and to love one another to walke in his wayes and to keepe his Commaundements and his Ordinance, and his lawes, and the Articles of our Covenant with him that wee may live and be multiplyed, and that the Lord our God may blesse us in the land whether wee goe to possesse it: . . .Therefore lett us choose life, that wee, and our Seede, may live; by obeyeing his voyce, and cleaveing to him, for hee is our life, and our prosperity.

PERSONAL NARRATIVE

Jonathan Edwards, 1739?

On January 12, 1723. I made a solemn dedication of myself to God, and wrote it down; giving up myself, and all that I had to God, to be for the future in no respect my own; to act as one that had no right to himself, in any respect. And solemnly vowed to take God for my whole portion and felicity; looking on nothing else as any part of my happiness, nor acting as if it were; and his law for the constant rule of my obedience; engaging to fight with all my might, against the world, the flesh and the devil, to the end of my life. . . .

I had great longings for the advancement of Christ's kingdom in the world; and my secret prayer used to be, in great part, taken up in praying for it. If I heard the least hint of any thing that happened, in any part of the world, that appeared, in some respect or other, to have a favorable aspect on the interest of Christ's kingdom, my soul eagerly catched at it; and it would much animate and refresh me. I used to be eager to read public news letters, mainly for that end; to see if I could not find some news favorable to the interest of religion in the world.

I very frequently used to retire into a solitary place, on the banks of Hudson's river, at some distance from the city, for contemplation on divine things, and secret converse with God; and had many sweet hours there. Sometimes Mr. Smith and I walked there together, to converse on the things of God; and our conversation used to turn much on the advancement of Christ's kingdom in the world, and the glorious things that God would accomplish for his church in the latter days. I had then, and at other times the greatest delight in the holy scriptures, of any book whatsoever. Oftentimes in reading it, every word seemed to touch my heart. I felt a harmony between something in my heart, and those sweet and powerful words. I seemed often to see so much light exhibited by every sentence, and such a refreshing food communicated, that I could not get along in reading; often dwelling long on one sentence, to see the wonders contained in it; and yet almost every sentence seemed to be full of wonders.

Jonathan Edwards, born in 1703 in Windsor, Connecticut, was the descendant of Puritans. A deeply religious man all of his life, in the mid-1700s, Edwards became a leader in the Great Awakening, which was a revival of religious fervor—in colonies up and down the eastern seaboard—in reaction to several generations of backsliding from the piety of the original Puritan settlers. Edwards's Personal Narrative *is a testament to the deep faith that governed his every thought and every action.*

PAINTING ABOVE: [64.456]
QUAKER MEETING (VARIANT OF A PAINTING ENTITLED
GRACECHURCH STREET MEETING, SOCIETY OF FRIENDS)
LATE-EIGHTEENTH OR EARLY-NINETEENTH CENTURY
ARTIST UNKNOWN
OIL ON CANVAS
25¼ X 30 INCHES
BEQUEST OF MAXIM KAROLIK
MUSEUM OF FINE ARTS
BOSTON, MASSACHUSETTS

William Penn was granted a large tract of land in America by the king of England as repayment of a debt owed by the king to Penn's father. The younger Penn, a devout Quaker who had been imprisoned in England several times for his outspoken religious views, used the land, along with adjacent territory purchased from the Delaware Indians, to found the colony of Pennsylvania. As leader of Pennsylvania, Penn never forgot the religious persecution he had suffered in England. He made certain that in his colony both political and religious freedom were granted to all citizens. William Penn was the first to draft a charter in America guaranteeing the separation of church and state, beginning a tradition of freedom of worship that remains a basic part of the American way of life today.

We are now remaining being in good health, and all our men well contented, free from mutinies, in love with one another; and as we hope in continual peace with the Indians, where we doubt not, by God's gracious assistance and the adventurer's willing mind and speedy furtherance to so honorable action, in after times to see our nation to enjoy a country not only exceeding pleasant for habitation but also very profitable for commerce in general, no doubt pleasing to almighty God, honorable to our gracious sovereign, commodious generally to the whole Kingdom.

John Smith

It is admirable to consider the power of faith, by which all things are (almost) possible to be done; it can remove mountains (if need were); it hath stayed the course of the sun, raised the dead, cast out devils, reversed the order of nature, quenched the violence of the fire, made the water become firm footing for Peter to walk on. . . . Faith is not only thus potent, but it is so necessary that without faith there is no salvation; therefore with all our seekings and gettings, let us above all seek to obtain this pearl of price.

Anne Bradstreet
Meditations Divine and Moral

Now faith is the substance of things hoped for, the evidence of things not seen.

Hebrews 11:1

RIGHT:
DEPARTURE OF THE MAYFLOWER
LIBRARY OF CONGRESS

To every thing there is a season, and a time to every purpose under the heaven: A time to be born, and a time to die; a time to plant, and a time to pluck up that which is planted; A time to kill, and a time to heal; a time to break down, and a time to build up; . . .

Ecclesiastes 3:1-3

God of our weary years,
God of our silent tears,
Thou who hast brought us thus far on the way;
Thou who hast by Thy might,
Led us into the light,
Keep us forever in the path, we pray.

Lest our feet stray from the places, our God,
    where we met Thee,
Lest our hearts, drunk with the wine of the
    world, we forget Thee;
Shadowed beneath Thy hand,
    may we forever stand,
True to our God, true to our native land.

James Weldon Johnson
and J. Rosamond Johnson
"Lift Ev'ry Voice and Sing," 1900

"Lift Ev'ry Voice and Sing" was known as the "Negro National Anthem" in the early 1900s. It was written by brothers James and J. Rosamond Johnson to be sung at a celebration in honor of the birthday of Abraham Lincoln. Today virtually unknown, the song speaks of the great faith of all Americans through the many trials of life.

from THE JOURNAL OF MARGARET MORRIS

Dec 6th, 1776. Being on a visit to my friend, M. S., at Haddonfield, I was preparing to return to my family, when a person from Philadelphia told me the people there were in great commotion,—that the English fleet was in the river, and hourly expected to sail up to the city,—that the inhabitants were removing into the country,—and that several persons of considerable repute had been discovered to have formed a design of setting fire to the city, and were summoned before the congress and strictly enjoined to drop the horrid purpose. When I heard the above report my heart almost died within me, and I cried, surely the Lord will not punish the innocent with the guilty, and I wished there might be found some interceding Lots and Abrahams amongst our people. On my journey home, I was told the inhabitants of our little town [Burlington, N.J.] were going in haste into the country, and that my nearest neighbours were already removed. When I heard this, I felt myself quite sick; I was ready to faint—I thought of my S. D. the beloved companion of my widowed state—her husband at the distance of some hundred miles from her—I thought of my own lonely situation, no husband to cheer with the voice of love my sinking spirits. My little flock, too, without a father to direct them how to steer. All these things crowded into my mind at once, and I felt like one forsaken; a flood of friendly tears came to my relief, and I felt a humble confidence that He who had been with me in six troubles, would not forsake me now. While I cherished this hope, my tranquility was restored, and I felt no sensations but of humble acquiescence to the Divine will—and was favoured to find my family in good health on my arrival, and my dear companion not greatly discomposed, for which favour I desire to be truly thankful.

Margaret Morris, like most colonial American women and children, did not fight in the actual battles for American independence, but nonetheless, her courage and faith were put to the test by the struggle. Alone and frightened by the battles raging ever closer to her home, Morris relied upon her faith to lead her through; this is a tradition that remains strong in America today. George Washington, pictured above with members of his own family in a respite from the roles of general and national hero, must also have relied upon his own personal faith and his thoughts of loved ones at home as he led the American colonies on the road to becoming the United States of America.

PORTRAIT LEFT:
JULIA WARD HOWE
(1819-1910)
BEGUN BY JOHN ELLIOTT (1858-1925); FINISHED BY WILLIAM HENRY COTTON (1880-1958)
OIL ON CANVAS
NATIONAL PORTRAIT GALLERY
SMITHSONIAN INSTITUTION

Julia Ward Howe was a northern poet inspired by the tragedy of the Civil War to write one of America's most enduring and beloved hymns. The text for "The Battle Hymn of the Republic"—sung to the tune of "John Brown's Body"—first appeared in the Atlantic Monthly *magazine in February of 1862; almost immediately, it was adopted as the unofficial anthem of the Union Army. Howe's song, however, was not about the battles of men on earth but of the battle fought by all Christians to see that God's work was done and His word obeyed. "The Battle Hymn of the Republic" did not belong to the soldiers of the North but to all Americans who held the fervent hope that peace would return to their land and justice would be secured. Praised by President Lincoln, "The Battle Hymn of the Republic" has remained a cherished part of American culture for more than one hundred years.*

BATTLE HYMN OF THE REPUBLIC

Julia Ward Howe, 1861

Mine eyes have seen the glory
Of the coming of the Lord;
He is trampling out the vintage
Where the grapes of wrath are stored;
He hath loosed the fateful lightning
Of His terrible swift sword:
His truth is marching on.

Glory! Glory! Hallelujah!
Glory! Glory! Glory! Hallelujah!
Glory! Glory! Hallelujah!
His truth is marching on.

I have seen Him in the watch-fires
Of a hundred circling camps;
They have builded him an altar
In the evening dews and damps;
I can read His righteous sentence
By the dim and flaring lamps:
His day is marching on.

Glory! Glory! Hallelujah!
Glory! Glory! Glory! Hallelujah!
Glory! Glory! Hallelujah!
His truth is marching on.

He has sounded forth the trumpet
That shall never call retreat;
He is sifting out the hearts of men
Before His judgment-seat:

Oh, be swift, my soul, to answer Him!
Be jubilant, my feet!
Our God is marching on.

Glory! Glory! Hallelujah!
Glory! Glory! Glory! Hallelujah!
Glory! Glory! Hallelujah!
His truth is marching on.

In the beauty of the lilies
Christ was born across the sea,
With a glory in his bosom that
Transfigures you and me:
As he died to make men holy,
Let us die to make men free,
While God is marching on.

Glory! Glory! Hallelujah!
Glory! Glory! Glory! Hallelujah!
Glory! Glory! Hallelujah!
His truth is marching on.

He is coming like the glory
Of the morning on the wave;
He is wisdom to the mighty,
He is honor to the brave;
So the world shall be His footstool,
And the soul of wrong His slave,
Our God is marching on.

A NATIONAL PRAYER

Thomas Jefferson

Almighty God, Who has given us this good land for our heritage, we humbly beseech Thee that we may always prove ourselves a people mindful of Thy favor and glad to do Thy will.

Bless our land with honorable industry,
sound learning, and pure manners.
Save us from violence, discord and confusion,
from pride and arrogance, and from every evil way.
Defend our liberties, and fashion into one united
people the multitude brought hither out of
many kindreds and tongues.

Endow with the spirit of wisdom those to whom
in Thy Name we entrust the authority of government,
that there may be justice and peace at home,
and that through obedience to Thy law, we may show
forth Thy praise among the nations of the earth.

In time of prosperity, fill our hearts with
thankfulness, and, in the day of trouble, suffer not
our trust in Thee to fail; all of which we ask through
Jesus Christ our Lord.
Amen.

The story of America is the story of the power of faith. We have gone from a handful of brave settlers to a country of billions; our belief in a higher power is as important today as has ever been to guide us through the joys and the trials of life. The American tradition of faith is one we must nurture and respect as we face the unknown future.

OUR SPIRIT OF INDUSTRY

I wish to preach not the doctrine of ignoble ease but the doctrine of the strenuous life; the life of toil and effort; of labor and strife; to preach that highest form of success which comes not to the man who desires mere easy peace but to the man who does not shrink from danger, from hardship, or from bitter toil, and who out of these wins the splendid ultimate triumph.

Theodore Roosevelt
The Strenuous Life

PAINTING ABOVE:
CHILMARK HAY
THOMAS HART BENTON (1889-1975)
© 1994 T.H. BENTON AND RITA P. BENTON TESTAMENTARY TRUSTS/VAGA, NY

A PSALM OF LIFE

Henry Wadsworth Longfellow

Tell me not, in mournful numbers,
    "Life is but an empty dream!"
    For the soul is dead that slumbers,
And things are not what they seem.

Life is real! Life is earnest!
    And the grave is not its goal;
"Dust thou art, to dust returnest,"
    Was not spoken of the soul.

Not enjoyment, and not sorrow,
    Is our destined end or way;
But to act, that each tomorrow
    Finds us farther than today.

Art is long, and Time is fleeting,
    And our hearts, though stout and brave,
Still, like muffled drums, are beating
    Funeral marches to the grave.

In the world's broad field of battle,
    In the bivouac of Life,

Be not like dumb, driven cattle!
    Be a hero in the strife!

Trust no Future, howe'er pleasant!
    Let the dead Past bury its dead!
Act,—act in the living Present!
    Heart within, and God o'erhead!

Lives of great men all remind us
    We can make our lives sublime,
And, departing, leave behind us
    Footprints on the sands of time;

Footprints, that perhaps another,
    Sailing o'er life's solemn main,
A forlorn and shipwrecked brother,
    Seeing, shall take heart again.

Let us, then, be up and doing,
    With a heart for any fate;
Still achieving, still pursuing,
    Learn to labor, and to wait.

PAINTING
RIGHT:
*FLAX
SCUTCHING
BEE*
LINCOLN PARK
(1826-1906)

from LETTERS FROM AN AMERICAN FARMER

J. Hector St. John de Crèvecoeur, 1782

I wish I could be acquainted with the feelings and thoughts which must agitate the heart and present themselves to the mind of an enlightened Englishman, when he first lands on this continent. He must greatly rejoice that he lived at a time to see this fair country discovered and settled; he must necessarily feel a share of national pride, when he views the chain of settlements which embellishes these extended shores. . . . Here he sees the industry of his native country displayed in a new manner, and traces in their works the embryos of all the arts, sciences, and ingenuity which flourish in Europe. Here he beholds fair cities, substantial villages, extensive fields, an immense country filled with decent houses, good roads, orchards, meadows, and bridges, where an hundred years ago all was wild, woody, and uncultivated! What a train of pleasing ideas this fair spectacle must suggest; it is a prospect that must inspire a good citizen with the most heartfelt pleasure. . . . Here are no aristocratical families, no courts, no kings, no bishops, no ecclesiastical dominion, no invisible power giving to a few a very visible one; no great manufacturers employing thousands, no great refinements of luxury. The rich and poor are not so far removed from each other as they are in Europe. Some few towns excepted, we are all tillers of the earth, from Nova Scotia to West Florida. We are a people of cultivators, scattered over an immense territory. . . .

PHOTOGRAPH LEFT:
PLOWING THE FIELD
ARCHIVE PHOTOS/LAMBERT

Nothing can exceed their activity and preservation in all kinds of speculation, handicraft, and enterprise which promise a profitable pecuniary result. . . . Such unity of purpose, such sympathy of feeling can, I believe, be found nowhere else, except, perhaps, in an ant's nest.

Francis Trollope
Domestic Matters of Americans, 1832

RIGHT:
SAWING INTO LOGS
LIBRARY OF CONGRESS

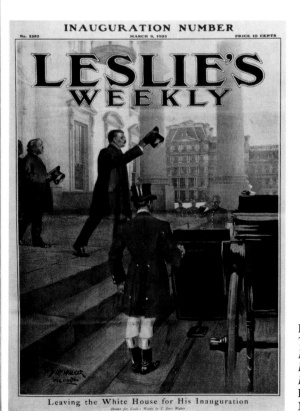

Associate with men of good quality if you esteem your own reputation; for it is better to be alone than in bad company.

George Washington

The first requisite of a good citizen in this Republic of ours is that he shall be able and willing to pull his weight.

Theodore Roosevelt

LEFT:
THEODORE ROOSEVELT
LEAVING THE WHITE
HOUSE FOR HIS
INAUGURATION
LESLIE'S WEEKLY
MARCH 9, 1905

In our hands is placed a power
  greater than their hoarded gold;
Greater than the might of armies
  magnified a thousand fold,
We can bring to birth a new world
  from the ashes of the old.
For the Union makes us strong.

Solidarity forever!
Solidarity forever!
Solidarity forever!
For the Union makes us strong.

Ralph Chaplin
"Solidarity Forever"

PHOTOGRAPH ABOVE:
WOMEN WORKERS IN WORLD WAR I
FPG INTERNATIONAL

Everything comes to him
who hustles while he waits.

Thomas A. Edison

There is no place in civilization for the idler. None of
us has any right to ease.

Henry Ford

PAINTING LEFT:
WISCONSIN PLANK ROAD, 1850
THORSTEN LINDBERG
MILWAUKEE COUNTY HISTORICAL
SOCIETY

from CROSSING BROOKLYN FERRY

Walt Whitman

Others will enter the gates of the ferry and cross
    from shore to shore,
    Others will watch the run of the flood-tide,
Others will see the shipping of Manhattan north and
    west, and the heights of Brooklyn to the south
      and east,
Others will see the islands large and small;
Fifty years hence, others will see them as they cross,
    the sun half an hour high,
A hundred years hence, or ever so many hundred years
    hence, others will see them.
Will enjoy the sunset, the pouring-in of the flood-tide,
    the falling-back to the sea of the ebb-tide.

The Brooklyn Bridge is a monumental tribute to the power of American industriousness. Construction began on the bridge on January 2, 1870. The bridge was designed to span the East River from Park Row in Manhattan to Washington Street in Brooklyn. The building process spanned thirteen years—and captured the imagination of the American people. John A. Roebling, the suspension bridge designer who planned Brooklyn's bridge, died in 1869, before formal construction had begun, after an accident on the building site. His son took over on-site supervision of the project until 1872, when a case of the bends caused by too much time in the underground caissons constructed to build the bridge tower forced him to work from his bed for the remainder of the project. When the bridge was completed in 1883, it spanned 1,595 feet and rose 272 feet to the sky on a foundation set 78 feet under the water level. The massive, spectacular bridge was a tribute to the countless individuals who had toiled to make it a reality, and to the belief that hard work, ingenuity, and perseverance can accomplish anything.

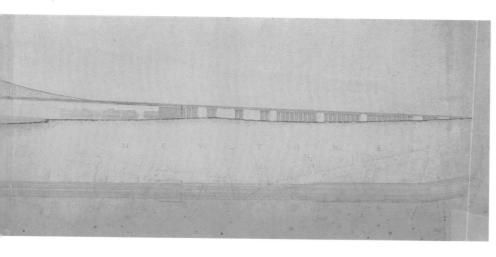

Painting above:
*A Winter Day on the
Brooklyn Bridge*
Childe Hassam (1859-1935)

I HEAR AMERICA SINGING

Walt Whitman

I hear America singing, the varied carols I hear,
   Those of mechanics, each one singing his as it should be blithe and strong,
   The carpenter singing his as he measures his plank or beam,
The mason singing his as he makes ready for work, or leaves off work,
The boatman singing what belongs to him in his boat, the deck-hand singing
      on the steamboat deck,
The shoemaker singing as he sits on his bench,
      the hatter singing as he stands,
The wood-cutter's song, the ploughboy's on his way in the morning,
      or at noon intermission or at sundown,
The delicious singing of the mother, or of the young wife at work,
      or of the girl sewing or washing,
Each singing what belongs to him or her and to none else,
The day what belongs to the day—at night the party of young
      fellows, robust, friendly,
Singing with open mouths their strong melodious songs.

AN IMMIGRANT PEDDLER

Morris Horowitz, as told to Hilda Polacheck, 1939

How did I happen to become a peddler? When I came to Chicago in 1870, there was nothing else to do. I was eighteen years old. I had learned no trade in Russia. The easiest thing to do was to peddle. People coming to America today have a much harder time. There are better houses to live in and nearly everybody has a bathtub, but there are no jobs. In the old days, if you had a few dollars, you could buy some dry goods and peddle. . . .

I went to live with an aunt and uncle when I first came to Chicago. They lived in a small four-room house on Fourth Avenue. They had four children but they managed to rent one room to two roomers. I shared the bed with these two men. The day after I got to Chicago my uncle asked me if I had any money. I told him I had ten dollars. He told me to invest it in dry goods and start peddling. . . . It was the great fire of 1871 that made me a country peddler. . . . Since many homes were burned, many people left the city. Some went to live with relatives in other cities. A great many men became country peddlers. There were thousands of men walking from farm to farm with heavy packs on their backs. These peddlers carried all kinds of merchandise, things they thought farmers and their families could use.

There was no rural mail delivery in those days. The farmers very seldom saw a newspaper and were hungry for news. They were very glad to see a peddler from any large city. They wanted to hear all about the great fire. When I told a farmer that I was from Chicago, he was very glad to see me. You see, I was a newspaper and a department store.

The farms were ten, fifteen, twenty, even thirty miles apart. It would take a day sometimes to walk from one farm to the next. . . . It was not an easy life, but we made pretty good money. Most of the men had come from Europe and had left their families behind. We were all trying to save enough money to bring relatives to America. . . .

After carrying my pack on my back for two years, I decided to buy a horse and wagon. Many other peddlers got the same idea. I used to meet the small covered wagons as they drove about the country. I had now been peddling for five years and had saved enough money to bring my father, brothers, and sisters to Chicago. . . .

I never got rich. My wife and I raised six children. When my sisters and brothers got married, my father came to live with us. Then one of my sisters died and her children came to live with us. Then my wife brought her parents to America and they lived with us. Then we wanted our children to have an education, so we sent them to college. There never was enough money left to start any kind of business. But I feel that we made a good investment.

Nobody understood the necessity, and the value, of hard work more than the millions of immigrants who came to America in the late nineteenth and early twentieth centuries looking for the opportunity to work toward a better life. Many came with nothing more than the clothes they were wearing, the name of one distant relative already at work on American soil, and a fierce determination to succeed; few spoke English or had money in their pockets for anything but a few days' food and lodging. But most found what they were looking for—the chance to become a hard-working, solid American citizen. Through all the years of her existence, America has learned that its newest citizens are often the most dedicated to the American way of life, and the most willing to work hard and long to achieve it.

LEFT:
VICTORY WAITS ON YOUR FINGERS
PHOTOLITHOGRAPH
PRODUCED BY THE ROYAL
TYPEWRITER COMPANY
FOR THE U.S. CIVIL SERVICE
COMMISSION
NATIONAL ARCHIVES

World War II brought serious labor shortages to America. Demands soared in the armed forces and the defense industries as well as in civilian business; all needed workers to fill the jobs left open by soldiers and to make the products necessary to support the war effort. Women had been entering the work force in increasing numbers in the middle of the twentieth century, but with the crisis of wartime, the country needed even greater numbers of women to go to work outside their homes. A massive public relations campaign was organized by the government to encourage and inspire women to get jobs—to help themselves and to help their country. From this campaign came the classic image of Rosie the Riveter: a strong, independent woman capable of filling jobs once thought the sole domain of American men. The campaign was a success; countless American women, many of whom had never held a job outside their home, went to work in factories and offices across the nation. When the war was over, many were reluctant to leave: the American woman was now a permanent presence in the workplace.

LEFT:
We Can Do It!
J. HOWARD MILLER
PHOTOLITHOGRAPH
PRODUCED BY
WESTINGHOUSE FOR
THE WAR PRODUCTION
CO-ORDINATING
COMMITTEE
NATIONAL ARCHIVES

BELOW:
It's Our Fight Too!
JACK CAMPBELL
PHOTOLITHOGRAPH
PRODUCED BY THE DOUGLAS AIRCRAFT
COMPANY
NATIONAL ARCHIVES

These jobs will have to be glorified as a patriotic war service if American women are to be persuaded to take them and stick to them. Their importance to a nation engaged in total war must be convincingly presented.

Basic Program Plan for Womanpower,
Office of War Information,
August 1943

LEFT:
LONGING WON'T BRING HIM BACK SOONER . . . GET A WAR JOB!
LAWRENCE WILBUR, 1944
PHOTOLITHOGRAPH
PRINTED BY THE GOVERNMENT PRINTING OFFICE FOR THE WAR MANPOWER COMMISSION
NATIONAL ARCHIVES

THE STRENUOUS LIFE

Theodore Roosevelt, 1899

I wish to preach not the doctrine of ignoble ease but the doctrine of the strenuous life; the life of toil and effort; of labor and strife; to preach that highest form of success which comes not to the man who desires mere easy peace but to the man who does not shrink from danger, from hardship, or from bitter toil, and who out of these wins the splendid ultimate triumph. . . .

As it is with the individual so it is with the nation. It is a base untruth to say that happy is the nation that has no history. Thrice happy is the nation that has a glorious history. Far better it is to dare mighty things, to win glorious triumphs, even though checkered by failure, than to take rank with those poor spirits who neither enjoy much nor suffer much because they live in the gray twilight that knows neither victory nor defeat. . . . The timid man, the lazy man, the man who distrusts his country, the overcivilized man, who has lost his great fighting, masterful virtues, the ignorant man and the man of dull mind, whose soul is incapable of feeling the mighty lift that thrills "stern men with empires in their brains"—all these, of course, shrink from seeing the nation undertake its new duties; shrink from seeing us build a navy and army adequate to our needs; shrink from seeing us do our share of the world's work by bringing order out of chaos. . . . These are the men who fear the strenuous life, who fear the only national life which is really worth leading.

PHOTOGRAPH LEFT:
THEODORE ROOSEVELT
TWENTY-SIXTH PRESIDENT OF THE
UNITED STATES
UNIDENTIFIED PHOTOGRAPHER
NATIONAL PORTRAIT GALLERY
SMITHSONIAN INSTITUTION

THE NEW FREEDOM

Woodrow Wilson, 1912

Theodore Roosevelt was a man of unmatched energy—a true believer in the value of hard work and industry. A sickly child, Roosevelt vowed to overcome his physical weakness to lead a full, active life. Before he became president, Roosevelt was a soldier, police chief, cattle rancher, governor of New York, and vice president. He was also father of six, an avid boxer, sailor, rider, and adventurer—the picture of the active, industrious, confident American.

The hope of the United States in the present and in the future is the same that it has always been: it is the hope and confidence that out of unknown homes will come men who will constitute themselves the masters of industry and of politics. The average hopefulness, the average welfare, the average enterprise, the average initiative, of the United States are the only things that make it rich. We are not rich because a few gentlemen direct our industry; we are rich because of our own intelligence and our own industry. America does not consist of men who get their names into the newspapers; America does not consist politically of the men who set themselves up to be political leaders; she does not consist of the men who do most of her talking,—they are important only so far as they speak for that great voiceless multitude of men who constitute the great body and the saving force of the nation. Nobody who cannot speak the common thought, who does not move by the common impulse, is the man to speak for America, or for any of her future purposes. Only he is fit to speak who knows the thoughts of the great body of citizens, the men who go about their business every day, the men who toil from morning till night, the men who go home tired in the evenings, the men who are carrying on the things we are so proud of.

PAINTING LEFT:
[1963.10]
ROBINSON, COLORADO, 1887
HARRY LEARNED
(1842-AFTER 1895)
OIL ON CANVAS
18¼ X 30½ INCHES
AMON CARTER
MUSEUM
FORT WORTH, TEXAS

THE LEGACY OF INGENUITY

It was about this time that I conceiv'd the bold and arduous Project of arriving at moral Perfection. I wish'd to live without committing any Fault at anytime; I would conquer all that either Natural Inclination, Custom, or Company might lead me into. As I knew, or thought I knew, what was right and wrong, I did not see why I might not always do the one and avoid the other.

*Benjamin Franklin
from* The Autobiography

PAINTING RIGHT:
FISHERMEN ON ROCKS
WINSLOW HOMER (1836-1910)

from THE AUTOBIOGRAPHY OF BENJAMIN FRANKLIN, 1784

It was about this time that I conceiv'd the bold and arduous Project of arriving at moral Perfection. I wish'd to live without committing any Fault at anytime; I would conquer all that either Natural Inclination, Custom, or Company might lead me into. As I knew, or thought I knew, what was right and wrong, I did not see why I might not *always* do the one and avoid the other. But I soon found I had undertaken a Task of more Difficulty than I had imagined: While my Care was employ'd in guarding against one Fault, I was often surpris'd by another. Habit took the Advantage of Inattention. Inclination was sometimes too strong for Reason. I concluded at length, that the mere speculative Conviction that it was our Interest to be completely virtuous, was not sufficient to prevent our Slipping, and that the contrary Habits must be broken and good Ones acquired and established, before we can have any Dependence on a steady uniform Rectitude of Conduct. For this purpose I therefore contriv'd the following Method.

In the various Enumerations of the moral Virtues I had met with in my Reading, I found the Catalogue more or less numerous, as different Writers included more or fewer Ideas under the same Name. Temperance, for Example, was by some confin'd to Eating and Drinking, while by others it was extended to mean moderating every other Pleasure, Appetite, Inclination or Passion, bodily or mental, even to our Avarice and Ambition. I propos'd to myself, for the sake of Clearness, to use rather more Names with fewer Ideas annex'd to each, than a few Names with more Ideas; and I included after Thirteen Names of Virtues all that at that time occur'd to me as necessary or desirable, and annex'd to each a short Precept, which fully express'd the Extent I gave to its Meaning.

These Names of Virtues with their Precepts were:

1. Temperance. *Eat not to Dulness. Drink not to Elevation.*

2. Silence. *Speak not but what may benefit others or your self. Avoid trifling Conversation.*

3. Order. *Let all your Things have their Places. Let each Part of your Business have its Time.*

4. Resolution. *Resolve to perform what you ought. Perform without fail what you resolve.*

5. Frugality. *Make no Expense but to do good to others or yourself: i.e. Waste nothing.*

6. Industry. *Lose no Time. Be always employ'd in something useful. Cut off all unnecessary Actions.*

7. Sincerity. *Use no hurtful Deceit. Think innocently and justly; and, if you speak; speak accordingly.*

8. Justice. *Wrong none, by doing Injuries or omitting the Benefits that are your Duty.*

9. Moderation. *Avoid Extremes. Forbear resenting Injuries so much as you think they deserve.*

10. Cleanliness. *Tolerate no Uncleanness in Body, Clothes or Habitation.*

11. Tranquility. *Be not disturbed at Trifles, or at Accidents common or unavoidable.*

12. Chastity. *Rarely use Venery but for Health or Offspring; never to Dulness, Weakness, or the Injury of your own or another's Peace or Reputation.*

13. Humility. *Imitate Jesus and Socrates.*

Benjamin Franklin so strongly believed in the value of hard work and diligence that he was not afraid to state in his autobiography that he set out to achieve a state of "moral perfection." But the lesson of Franklin's writings and his life is not how to achieve moral perfection, but the value of making the effort and the truly American belief that there is no limit to what can be accomplished with honest hard work and a little ingenuity.

RIGHT:
BENJAMIN FRANKLIN(1706-1790)
EDWARD SAVAGE (1761-1817)
MEZZOTINT
NATIONAL PORTRAIT GALLERY
SMITHSONIAN INSTITUTION

THE CASE FOR PUBLIC SCHOOLS

Horace Mann, 1848

Education, then, beyond all other devices of human origin, is the great equalizer of the conditions of men—the balance-wheel of the social machinery. I do not here mean that it so elevates the moral nature as to make men disdain and abhor the oppression of their fellow-men. This idea pertains to another of its attributes. But I mean that it gives each man the independence and the means, by which he can resist the selfishness of other men. It does better than to disarm the poor of their hostility toward the rich; it prevents being poor. . . . And so it is, not in one department only, but in the whole circle of human labors. The annihilation of the sun would no more certainly be followed by darkness, than the extinction of human intelligence would plunge the race at once into the weakness and helplessness of barbarism. To have created such beings as we are, and to have placed them in this world, without the light of the sun, would be no more cruel than for a government to suffer its laboring classes to grow up without knowledge.

Horace Mann (1796-1859) was a crusader for quality free public education in America. He was a man of great energy and commitment who once told a group of college students to "be ashamed to die until you have won some victory for humanity." As the secretary of the Massachusetts Board of Education, Mann was an innovator in the field of public education. At a time when many Americans did not believe in the absolute necessity of quality public education for all, Mann, more than any other single individual, defined the course of public education and worked to assure that it would be humane, inclusive, and thorough.

RIGHT:
HORACE MANN (1796-1859)
FRANCIS D'AVIGNON
LITHOGRAPH WITH TINTSTONE
NATIONAL PORTRAIT GALLERY
SMITHSONIAN INSTITUTION

George Washington Carver, born sometime around 1864 in Missouri, was a botanist and agricultural chemist, a brilliant pioneer in plant research best known for his innovative studies on the uses of the peanut. Carver discovered three-hundred different uses for the peanut and its by-products, including plastics, dye, milk substitutes, medicines, flour, fertilizer, coffee, and ink. He hoped that his research would rejuvenate farming in the South, where much land had been rendered almost useless by generations of cotton growing. Carver also had a great impact as a teacher at the Tuskegee Institute in Alabama. The school, founded by Booker T. Washington, opened July 4, 1881, with the mission of providing educational opportunity to black Americans. At Tuskegee, Carver shared his scientific genius with generations of young black students and with the farmers in the surrounding communities.

One of the great American inventors, Carver never sought a patent for any of his work; he believed that as the subjects of his research were the creation of God and the property of all mankind, so did his inventions and innovations belong to all who might put them to use. Carver died in 1943, shortly after receiving an honorary doctorate degree from the University of Rochester in New York. The date of his death, January 5, was declared George Washington Carver Day by the United States government in honor of his great contributions to American life.

ALEXANDER GRAHAM BELL AND THE TELEPHONE

Alexander Graham Bell was working on a system for transmitting electric telegraph signals simultaneously over one line when he came upon the means for transmitting speech. The patent issued to him on March 7, 1876, preceded his historic first telephone conversation by three days; on March 10, Bell spoke the first words via telephone. Patent drawings like the one below were required by law in order to secure a patent. The drawing, along with a written description of the invention, guaranteed that the exact nature of the invention was clear to all. In the more than one hundred years since its creation, Bell's invention has grown from the simple device pictured here to a worldwide system of over 600 million telephones that has truly revolutionized the way we live and work.

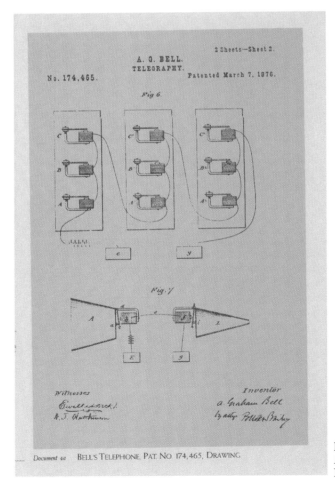

THOMAS EDISON AND THE ELECTRIC LIGHT

Before Thomas Edison made the electric light a viable commercial alternative to gas, kerosene, and the candle, lighting one's home was not safe, economical, or convenient. The idea of the incandescent lamp was not new, but it was Edison who made the necessary adjustments and innovations to make it practical. The patent drawing at right, submitted on January 27, 1880, appears remarkably simple; yet within this small drawing are the makings of a revolution in American life—and life throughout the world.

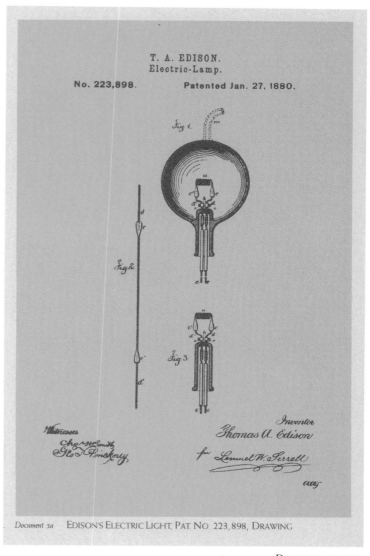

Document 5a   EDISON'S ELECTRIC LIGHT, PAT. NO. 223,898, DRAWING

DRAWING ABOVE:
EDISON'S ELECTRIC LIGHT,
PAT. NO. 223, 898, DRAWING
NATIONAL ARCHIVES AND
RECORDS ADMINISTRATION

PORTRAIT LEFT:
THOMAS EDISON (1847-1931)
A. ANDERSON
NATIONAL PORTRAIT GALLERY
SMITHSONIAN INSTITUTION

The man who has seen the rising moon break out of the clouds at midnight has been present . . . at the creation of light and the world.

Ralph Waldo Emerson

The most beautiful thing we can experience is the mysterious. It is the source of all true art and science.

Albert Einstein

Invention breeds invention.

Ralph Waldo Emerson

Few men during their lifetime come anywhere near exhausting the resources dwelling within them. There are deep wells of strength that are never used.

Admiral Richard Byrd

If you would have your son be something in the world, teach him to depend upon himself. Let him learn that it is by close and strenuous personal application that he must rise—that he must, in short, make himself, and be the architect of his own fortune.

Harry Edwards

The coaches that carried passengers and mail and helped America expand westward were, for the most part, manufactured in Concord, New Hampshire. The Concord Coach featured an innovative design with leather braces to replace the usual metal springs—providing the passengers with a much smoother ride. The coach pictured here was manufactured by Abbot and Downing of Concord in 1891 and was used for the transport of mail.

PHOTO LEFT:
CONCORD COACH
GREENFIELD VILLAGE

PAINTING
LEFT:
*THE ROBERT
E. LEE*
ST. LOUIS
MERCANTILE
LIBRARY
ST. LOUIS,
MISSOURI

from THE WRITINGS OF ORVILLE WRIGHT

The ground under you is at first a perfect blur, but as you rise the objects become clearer. At a height of one hundred feet you feel hardly any motion at all, except for the wind which strikes your face.

The operator moves a lever: the right wing rises, the machine swings about to the left. You make a very short turn, yet you do not feel the sensation of being thrown from your seat, so often experienced in automobile and railway travel. The objects on the ground now seem to be moving at much higher speed, though you perceive no change in the pressure of the wind on your face. You know then that you are traveling with the wind.

When you near the starting point, the operator stops the motor while still high in the air. The machine coasts down at an oblique angle to the ground, and after sliding fifty or a hundred feet comes to rest. The motor close beside you kept up an almost deafening roar during the whole flight, yet in your excitement you did not notice it until it stopped!

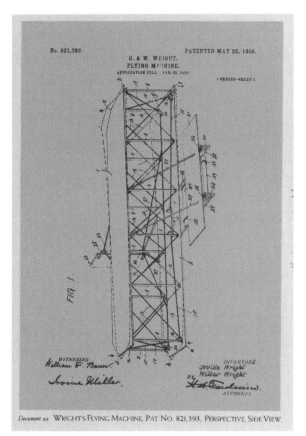

DRAWING ABOVE:
WRIGHT'S FLYING MACHINE,
PAT. NO. 821, 393
PERSPECTIVE, SIDE VIEW
NATIONAL ARCHIVES

The Wright brothers' patent number 821, 393—applied for in 1903—was for an unpowered glider. Only after the glider was perfected did they add the propeller and engine necessary for the first powered aircraft, which succeeded later that same year. One of the greatest inventions of all time, the airplane brought infinite changes to society. Life as we know it today would be entirely unthinkable without the airplane, which has made our entire nation—and our world— accessible to all.

PHOTOGRAPH LEFT:
EARLY FLIGHT
ARCHIVE PHOTOS/LAMBERT

PHOTOGRAPH ABOVE:
WRIGHT BROTHERS' FLIGHT AT KITTY HAWK, 1903
FPG INTERNATIONAL

HIGH FLIGHT

John Gillespie Magee, Jr., c.1940

Oh! I have slipped the surly bonds of Earth
   And danced the skies on laughter-silvered wings;
     Sunward I've climbed, and joined the tumbling mirth
  Of sun-split clouds,—and done a hundred things
You have not dreamed of—wheeled and soared and swung
  High in the sunlit silence. Hov'ring there,
I've chased the shouting wind along, and flung
  My eager craft through footless halls of air. . . .

Up, up the long, delirious, burning blue
  I've topped the wind-swept heights with easy grace,
Where never lark, or even eagle flew—
  And, while with silent lifting mind I've trod
  The high untrespasssed sanctity of space,
Put out my hand and touched the face of God.

The poem "High Flight" was written by John Gillespie Magee, Jr., an American citizen who fought in World War II with the Royal Canadian Air Force. Magee wrote the poem sometime between 1939 and 1941 and sent it to his parents in Washington, D.C. Magee did not return from the war; he was killed in flight in 1941.

PHOTOGRAPH ABOVE:
FORD ASSEMBLY LINE
FPG INTERNATIONAL/PHOTOWORLD

from **THE NEW FREEDOM**

Woodrow Wilson

You know how it thrills our blood sometimes to think how all the nations of the earth wait to see what America is going to do with her power, her physical power, her enormous resources, her enormous wealth. The nations hold their breath to see what this young country will do with her young unspoiled strength; we cannot help but be proud that we are strong. But what has made us strong? The toil of millions of men, the toil of men who do not boast, who are inconspicuous, but who live their lives humbly from day to day; it is the great body of toilers that constitutes the might of America.

Perhaps no single invention has transformed everyday American life so completely as the automobile. Behind the wheels of their cars Americans found a new freedom, unimaginable in the days when travel meant dependence upon horses or on train schedules. The first American patent for a gasoline-driven automobile was issued in June of 1895 to Charles E. Duryea of Chicopee, Massachusetts. Duryea and his brother Frank had conducted the first successful test of their vehicle inside a warehouse building because they feared the ridicule their invention would inspire in a skeptical public. The true automobile revolution was still a few years off, however; it was not until after World War I that Henry Ford introduced assembly line production to the manufacture of automobiles. Before then, each car was assembled individually, and the price was far out of the reach of the average American. Ford's assembly line cut production time of a Model T to one-and-one-half hours and cut prices to a level where the automobile became an affordable luxury for many families. In 1926 four million cars rolled off the Ford assembly line, and the transformation of America into an automobile-driven society was begun.

PHOTOGRAPH BELOW:
EARLY AUTOMOBILE, 1915
LIBRARY OF CONGRESS PHOTO

THE LIGHT OF CREATIVITY

The Americans, of all nations at any time upon the earth, have probably the fullest, poetical nature. The United States themselves are essentially the greatest poem. . . . Here is not merely a nation but a teeming nation of nations. . . . Here is the hospitality which forever indicates heroes.

Walt Whitman

PAINTING ABOVE:
OLD ELM AT MEDFIELD
GEORGE INNESS (1825-1894)

TO MY DEAR AND LOVING HUSBAND

Anne Bradstreet, 1666

If ever two were one, then surely we.
If ever man were lov'd by wife, then thee;
If ever wife was happy in a man,
Compare with me ye women if you can.
I prize thy love more than whole Mines of gold,
Or all the riches that the East doth hold.
My love is such that Rivers cannot quench,
Nor ought but love from thee, give recompence.
Thy love is such I can no way repay,
The heavens reward thee manifold I pray.
Then while we live, in love lets so persever,
That when we live no more, we may live ever.

Anne Bradstreet was one of America's first poetic voices. She came to the New World from England at the age of eighteen—among the first settlers of Massachusetts Bay Colony—along with her husband and her father, both leaders in the Puritan community. Bradstreet's first efforts at poetry were skillful imitations of the most respected English male Puritan poets of the day. As the years passed, however, and as she began to make peace with the difficult life she had found in New England, Bradstreet found her own voice. In the 1600s, although it was virtually unheard of for a Puritan woman to write poetry, Anne Bradstreet wrote simple, moving verses about her faith, her family, and her life in New England, beginning a tradition of independent creative expression that remains strong in America today.

A printer, journalist, teacher, clerk, newspaper editor, and poet, Walt Whitman celebrated the American creative spirit. Born on Long Island, New York, in 1819 and raised in Brooklyn, Whitman was in his mid-thirties when he published, at his own expense, nine hundred copies of a collection of poems he called Leaves of Grass. *The book gained little notice, but in years to come it—and his countless other poems—would be recognized for their innovative use of free verse and their intensely personal manner of expression. For generations, Whitman has been acknowledged as one of our greatest national treasures, a man with a unique, and truly American, creative genius. The poem below, "O Captain! My Captain!" appeared first in Whitman's collection* Sequel to Drum-Taps *in 1865, soon after the assassination of President Lincoln.*

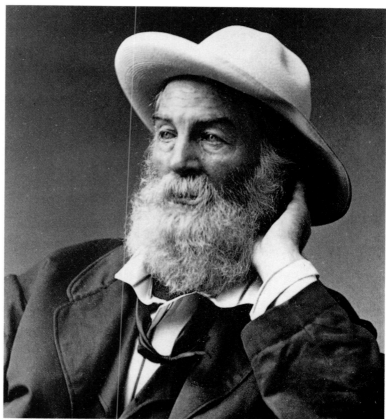

O CAPTAIN! MY CAPTAIN!

Walt Whitman, 1865

O Captain! my Captain! our fearful trip is done,
The ship has weather'd every rack, the prize we sought is won,
The port is near, the bells I hear, the people all exulting,
While follow eyes the steady keel, the vessel grim and daring;
    But O heart! heart! heart!
        O the bleeding drops of red,
           Where on the deck my Captain lies,
             Fallen cold and dead

O Captain! my Captain! rise up and hear the bells;
Rise up—for you the flag is flung—for you the bugle trills,
For you bouquets and ribbon'd wreaths—for you the shores a-crowding,
For you they call, the swaying mass, their eager faces turning;
    Here Captain! dear father!
        This arm beneath your head!
           It is some dream that on the deck,
             You've fallen cold and dead.

My Captain does not answer, his lips are pale and still,
My father does not feel my arm, he has no pulse nor will,
The ship is anchor'd safe and sound, its voyage closed and done,
From fearful trip the victor ship comes in with object won:
    Exult O shores, and ring O bells!
        But I with mournful tread,
           Walk the deck my Captain lies,
             Fallen cold and dead.

Legend has it that when Harriet Beecher Stowe visited President Lincoln at the White House in 1862, he greeted her saying, "So you are the little woman who wrote the book that made this great war!" Legend or not, however, Stowe's classic, Uncle Tom's Cabin, *opened the eyes of Americans to the true horrors of slavery and brought the issue to the forefront of the minds of many who had previously chosen to ignore it. Although critics have often found the novel lacking stylistically, none will deny that Stowe used her creative vision to inspire her readers to see things in a different light and in so doing made an undeniable mark on the progress of American history.*

from UNCLE TOM'S CABIN

Harriet Beecher Stowe

The women went off to their cabins, and Tom sat alone, by the smouldering fire, that flickered up redly in his face.

The silver, fair-browed moon rose in the purple sky, and looked down, calm and silent, as God looks on the scene of misery and oppression,—looked calmly on the lone black man, as he sat, with his arms folded, and his Bible on his knee.

"Is God here?" Ah, how is it possible for the untaught heart to keep its faith, unswerving, in the face of dire misrule, and palpable, unrebuked injustice? In that simple heart waged a fierce conflict: the crushing sense of wrong, the foreshadowing of a whole life of future misery, the wreck of all past hopes, mournfully tossing in the soul's sight. . . . Tom rose, disconsolate, and stumbled into the cabin that had been allotted to him. The floor was already strewn with weary sleepers, and the foul air of the place almost repelled him; but the heavy night-dews were chill, and his limbs weary, and, wrapping about him a tattered blanket, which formed his only bed-clothing, he stretched himself in the straw and fell asleep.

In dreams, a gentle voice came over his ear; . . . Eva, with her serious eyes bent downward, was reading to him from the Bible; and he heard her read:

"When thou passest through the waters, I will be with thee, and the rivers they shall not overflow thee; when thou walkest through the fire, thou shalt not be burned neither shall the flame kindle upon thee; for I am the Lord thy God, the Holy One of Israel, thy Saviour." . . .

Tom woke. Was it a dream? Let it pass for one. But who shall say that the sweet young spirit, which in life so yearned to comfort and console the distressed, was forbidden of God to assume this ministry after death?

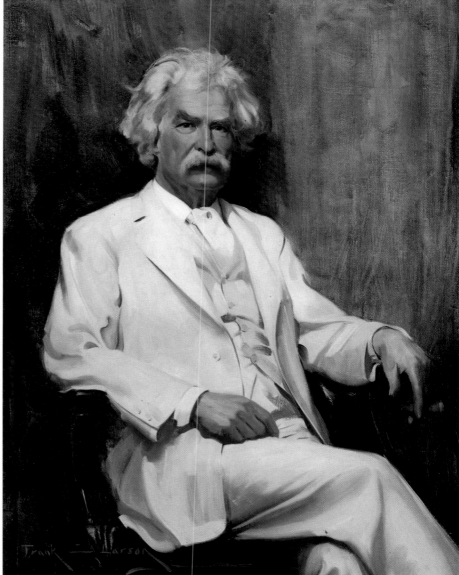

Mark Twain, born Samuel Langhorne Clemens in 1835, lived a colorful, active life. At various times a printer, a riverboat pilot on the Mississippi, a soldier, a miner, a reporter, and most memorably, a writer, Twain was a gifted storyteller and humorist who is counted among the greatest American authors. His pen name, taken from the jargon of his riverboat days, is known throughout the world, as are his classic stories about American life. Twain, who once called a classic a book that "everybody wants to have read and nobody wants to read," wrote with a wry sense of humor, a wonderful ear for local dialects, and a true understanding of the thoughts and dreams of the common American.

from ADVENTURES OF HUCKLEBERRY FINN

Mark Twain

You don't know me, without you have read a book by the name of "The Adventures of Tom Sawyer," but that ain't no matter. That book was made by Mr. Mark Twain, and he told the truth, mainly. There was things which he stretched, but mainly he told the truth. That is nothing. I never seen anybody but lied, one time or another, without it was Aunt Polly, or the widow, or maybe Mary. Aunt Polly—Tom's Aunt Polly, she is—and Mary, and the Widow Douglas, is all told about in that book—which is mostly a true book; with some stretchers, as I said before.

SELF-RELIANCE

Ralph Waldo Emerson, 1841

There is a time in every man's education when he arrives at the conviction that envy is ignorance; that imitation is suicide; that he must take himself for better for worse as his portion; that though the wide universe is full of good, no kernel of nourishing corn can come to him but through his toil bestowed on that plot of ground which is given to him to till. The power which resides in him is new in nature, and none but he knows what that is which he can do, nor does he know until he has tried. Not for nothing one face, one character, one fact, makes much impression on him, and another none. It is not without preestablished harmony, this sculpture in the memory. The eye was placed where one ray should fall, that it might testify of that particular ray. Bravely let him speak the utmost syllable of his confession. We but half express ourselves, and are ashamed of that divine idea which each of us represents. It may be safely trusted as proportionate and of good issues, so it be faithfully imparted, but God will not have his work made manifest by cowards. It needs a divine man to exhibit anything divine. A man is relieved and gay when he has put his heart into his work and done his best; but what he has said or done otherwise shall give him no peace. . . .

A foolish consistency is the hobgoblin of little minds, adored by little statesmen and philosophers and divines. With consistency a great soul has simply nothing to do. He may as well concern himself with his shadow on the wall. Out upon your guarded lips! Sew them up with packthread, do. Else if you would be a man speak what you think today in words as hard as cannon balls, and tomorrow speak what tomorrow thinks in hard words again, though it contradict everything you said today. Ah, then, exclaim the aged ladies, you shall be sure to be misunderstood! Misunderstood! It is a right fool's word. Is it so bad then to be misunderstood? Pythagoras was misunderstood, and Socrates, and Jesus, and Luther, and Copernicus, and Galileo, and Newton, and every pure and wise spirit that ever took flesh. To be great is to be misunderstood. . . .

THE AMERICAN SCHOLAR

Ralph Waldo Emerson

Mr. President and Gentlemen, this confidence in the unsearched might of man belongs, by all motives, by all prophecy, by all preparation, to the American Scholar. We have listened too long to the courtly muses of Europe. The spirit of the American freeman is already suspected to be timid, imitative, tame. . . . Young men of the fairest promise, who begin life upon our shores, inflated by the mountain winds, shined upon by all the stars of God, find the earth below not in unison with these, but are hindered from action by the disgust which the principles on which business is managed inspire. . . . What is the remedy? They did not yet see, and thousands of young men as hopeful now crowding to the barriers for the career do not yet see, that if the single man plant himself indomitably on his instincts, and there abide, the huge world will come round to him. Patience,—patience; with the shades of all the good and great for company; and for solace, the perspective of your own infinite life; and for work the study and the communication of principles, the making those instincts prevalent, the conversion of the world. Is it not the chief disgrace in the world, not to be an unit;—not to be reckoned one character;—not to yield that peculiar fruit which each man was created to bear, but to be reckoned in the gross, in the hundred, or the thousand, of the party, the section, to which we belong; and our opinion predicted geographically, as the north, or the south? Not so, brothers and friends— please God, ours shall not be so. We will walk on our own feet; we will work with our own hands; we will speak our own minds. The study of letters shall be no longer a name for pity, for doubt, and for sensual indulgence. The dread of man and the love of man shall be a wall of defence and a wreath of joy around all. A nation of men will for the first time exist, because each believes himself inspired by the Divine Soul which also inspires all men.

The Americans of all nations at any time upon the earth have probably the fullest poetical nature. The United States themselves are essentially the greatest poem. . . . Here is not merely a nation but a teeming nation of nations. . . . Here is the hospitality which forever indicates heroes.

Walt Whitman

Born in Canton, New York, in 1861 and educated at Yale, Frederic Remington fell in love with the West as a young man and made his life there as one of the most successful painters of the late nineteenth century. In a life fewer than fifty years long, Remington produced more than three thousand works of art, most of which celebrate his adopted home, what he called the "grand, silent country" of the American West.

PAINTING LEFT: [1961.232]
THE OLD STAGE COACH OF THE PLAINS, 1901
FREDERIC S. REMINGTON (1861-1909)
OIL ON CANVAS
40¼ X 27¼ INCHES
AMON CARTER MUSEUM
FORT WORTH, TEXAS

PAINTING BELOW: [33-4/4]
FISHING ON THE MISSISSIPPI, 1851
OIL ON CANVAS, 28¹¹⁄₁₆ X 37⅞ INCHES
GEORGE CALEB BINGHAM (1811-1879)
THE NELSON-ATKINS MUSEUM OF ART
KANSAS CITY, MISSOURI

George Caleb Bingham was a native of Augusta County, Virginia, but he made his name as a painter of the Missouri frontier. Bingham's family left Virginia when he was eight years old and traveled west to the town of Boon's Lick, Missouri. George Caleb Bingham was originally apprenticed to a cabinetmaker, but he discovered at a young age that his true talent was for painting. By the time he reached his thirties, Bingham was known across America for his paintings of western scenes—not grand and dramatic landscapes—but beautifully captured moments from the lives of the people who made their homes on the towns along the Missouri frontier.

The voice that beautifies the land!
The voice above, the voice of thunder,
Among the dark clouds again and again it sounds,
The voice that beautifies the land.

The voice that beautifies the land!
The voice below, the voice of the grasshopper,
Among the flowers and grasses again and again it sounds,
The voice that beautifies the land.

Navajo Prayer

I believe that a leaf of grass is no less than the journey-work of the stars, and the pismire is equally perfect, and a grain of sand, and the egg of the wren, and the tree-toad is a chef-d'oeuvre for the highest, and the running blackberry would adorn the parlors of heaven, and the narrowest hinge in my hand puts to scorn all machinery, and the cow crunching with depress'd head surpasses any statue, and a mouse is miracle enough to stagger sextillions of infidels.

Walt Whitman

All things in this world must be seen with the morning dew on them, must be seen with youthful, early-opened, hopeful eyes.

Henry David Thoreau

Climb the mountains and get their good tidings. Nature's peace will flow into you as sunshine flows into trees. The winds will flow their own freshness into you, and the storms their energy, while cares will drop away from you like the leaves of autumn.

John Muir

PAINTING LEFT:
*MARY STEVENSON
CASSATT* (1845-1926)
EDGAR DEGAS (1834-
1917)
OIL ON CANVAS
NATIONAL PORTRAIT
GALLERY
SMITHSONIAN
INSTITUTION

The artist who painted this portrait of Mary Cassatt, impressionist Edgar Degas, once remarked of her work: "I will not admit that a woman can draw like that." Degas did not hold that opinion for long, however; he and the other leading male painters of the late nineteenth century soon welcomed the young, talented Cassatt into their midst as an equal. Cassatt had faced doubters before: her own father objected to her artistic ambitions, but she persevered nonetheless and graduated from the Pennsylvania Academy of the Fine Arts in 1865 at the age of twenty-one. Within a few years she was living in Paris and counted among the most skilled American painters of her day. Her most lasting and cherished works are her portraits of mother and child—sensitive, elegant paintings that portray all the grace and beauty of their subject matter.

THE ETERNAL GOODNESS
John Greenleaf Whittier

I know not what the future hath
　Of marvel or surprise;
Assured alone that life and death
　His mercy underlies.

And if my heart and flesh are weak
　To bear an untried pain,
The bruised reed He will not break,
　But strengthen and sustain.

No offerings of my own I have,
　No works my faith to prove;

I can but give the gifts he gave,
　And plead His love for love.

And so, beside the silent sea,
　I wait the muffled oar;
No harm from Him can come to me
　On ocean or on shore.

I know not where His islands lift
　Their fronded palms in air;
I only know I cannot drift
　Beyond His love and care.

PAINTING ABOVE: [1970.252]
MOTHER AND CHILD, ABOUT 1902
MARY STEVENSON CASSATT (1845-1926)
OIL ON CANVAS, 36½ X 29 INCHES

GIFT OF MISS AIMÉE LAMB IN MEMORY OF
MR. AND MRS. HORATIO A. LAMB
MUSEUM OF FINE ARTS
BOSTON, MASSACHUSETTS

AN INHERITANCE OF EMPATHY

*"Keep, ancient lands,
your storied pomp!" cries she
With silent lips, "Give me
your tired, your poor,
Your huddled masses
yearning to breathe free,
The wretched refuse
of your teeming shore.
Send these, the homeless,
tempest-tost to me,
I lift my lamp
beside the golden door!"*

*Emma Lazarus
from "The New Colossus"*

PAINTING ABOVE:
HOUSE IN THE WOODS
ALBERT BIERSTADT (1830-1902)

PAINTING ABOVE: [64.450]
BATTLE OF GETTYSBURG
DAVID GILMOUR BLYTHE
(1815-1865)
OIL ON CANVAS
26 X 34½ INCHES
BEQUEST OF MAXIM
KAROLIK
MUSEUM OF FINE ARTS
BOSTON,
MASSACHUSETTS

Unlike William Lloyd Garrison, John Woolman was not a public leader of the abolition movement; rather, he was, like countless other Americans of every era, a quiet spokesperson for the humanitarian spirit by which we all seek to live. An eighteenth-century New Jersey Quaker, Woolman was devoted to living a life of good conscience. He often traveled to other Quaker communities and spoke on issues such as slavery, prejudice, and the treatment of the Indians. His journal was not published until after his death; it was, however, written with public readership in mind. Woolman, who lived a thoughtful, quiet life, hoped that others would be inspired by his writing to make empathy and spirituality a part of their everyday lives.

PROSPECTUS FOR THE LIBERATOR

William Lloyd Garrison, 1831

I am aware that many object to the severity of my language; but is there not cause for severity? I *will be* as harsh as truth, and as uncompromising as justice. On this subject, I do not wish to think, or speak, or write, with moderation. No! no! Tell a man whose house is on fire, to give a moderate alarm; tell him to moderately rescue his wife from the hands of the ravisher; tell the mother to gradually extricate her babe from the fire into which it has fallen;—but urge me not to use moderation in a cause like the present. I am in earnest—I will not equivocate—I will not excuse—I will not retreat a single inch—AND I WILL BE HEARD. The apathy of the people is enough to make every statue leap from its pedestal, and to hasten the resurrection of the dead.

It is pretended, that I am retarding the cause of emancipation, by the coarseness of my invective, and the precipitancy of my measures. *The charge is not true.* On this question my influence,—humble as it is,—is felt at this moment to a considerable extent, and shall be felt in coming years—not perniciously, but beneficially—not as a curse, but as a blessing; and posterity will bear testimony that I was right. I desire to thank God, that he enables me to disregard "the fear of man which bringeth a snare," and to speak his truth in its simplicity and power. . . .

William Lloyd Garrison was a powerful, passionate abolitionist who believed that an absolute and immediate end to slavery was the only righteous course for America to take. A Massachusetts journalist, Garrison also worked for the causes of women's rights and pacifism. At a time when it was easy for white northerners to simply ignore the issue of southern slavery, Garrison could not blind himself to the suffering of others. The Liberator *was the abolition newspaper he founded in 1831. He went on to found the New England Anti-Slavery Society and the American Anti-Slavery Society. The lines of his* Prospectus *are a testament to the passion with which he took up the cause of abolition, and also the sensitivity and integrity which governed the course of his life.*

from THE JOURNAL AND ESSAYS OF JOHN WOOLMAN, 1774

My Employer having a Negro woman sold her, and directed me to write a bill of Sale, The man being waiting who had bought her. The thing was Sudden, and though the thoughts of writing an Instrument of Slavery for one of my fellow creatures felt uneasie, yet I remembered I was hired by the year; that it was my master who directed me to do it, and that it was an Elderly man, a member of our society [of Quaker Friends] who bought her, so through weakness I gave way, and wrote it, but at the Executing it I was so Afflicted in my mind, that I said before my Master and the friend, that I believed Slavekeeping to be a practice inconsistent with the Christian Religion: this in some degree abated my uneasiness, yet as often as I reflected seriously upon it I thought I should have been clearer, if I had desired to be Excused from it, as a thing against my conscience, for such it was. [And] some time after this a young man of our Society, spoke to me to write [an instrument of Slavery], he having taken a Negro into his house. I told him I was not easie to write it, for though many [people] kept slaves in our society as in others, I still believed the practice was not right, and desired to be excused from doing the writing. I spoke to him in good will, and he told me, that keeping slaves was not altogether agreable to his mind, but that the slave being a gift made to his wife, he had accepted of her.

Great Spirit, help me to never judge another until I have walked in his moccasins for two weeks.

Sioux Prayer

With malice toward none, with charity for all, with firmness in the right as God gives us to see the right, let us strive on to finish the work we are in: to bind up the nation's wounds; to care for him who shall have borne the battle and for his widow and his orphan, to do all which may achieve and cherish a just and lasting peace among ourselves and with all nations.

Abraham Lincoln
Second Inaugural Address
March, 1865

Every man takes care that his neighbor doesn't cheat him. But a day comes when he begins to care that he does not cheat his neighbor. Then all goes well.

Ralph Waldo Emerson

PHOTOGRAPH ABOVE:
CAMPAIGN BUTTON OF ABRAHAM LINCOLN
DATE UNKNOWN

It is for them to honor principles rather than men—to commemorate events rather than days; when they rejoice, to know for what they rejoice, and to rejoice only for what has brought and what brings peace and happiness to men. The event we commemorate this day has procured much of both, and shall procure in the onward course of human improvement more than we can now conceive of. For this—for the good obtained and yet in store for our race—let us rejoice! But let us rejoice as men, not as children—as human beings rather than as Americans—as reasoning beings, not as ignorants. So shall we rejoice to good purpose and in good feeling; so shall we improve the victory once on this day achieved, until all mankind hold with us the Jubilee of Independence.

Frances Wright
The Meaning of Patriotism in America, July 4, 1828

Whatever America hopes to bring to pass in the world must first come to pass in the heart of America. The peace we seek, then, is nothing less than the fulfillment of our whole faith, among ourselves and in our dealings with others.

This signifies more than the stilling of guns, easing the sorrow of war. More than escape from death, it is a way of life. More than a haven for the weary, it is a hope for the brave.

This is the hope that beckons us onward. . . . This is the work that awaits us all. To be done with bravery, and charity, and with Prayer to Almighty God.

Dwight D. Eisenhower

PHOTOGRAPH ABOVE:
CAMPAIGN BUTTON FOR DWIGHT DAVID EISENHOWER
1952

Beautiful faces are they that wear
The light of a pleasant spirit there;
Beautiful hands are they that do
Deeds that are noble, good, and true;
Beautiful feet are they that go
Swiftly to lighten another's woe.

McGuffey's Second Reader

LEFT:
WILLIAM PENN'S TREATY WITH THE INDIANS WHEN HE FOUNDED PENNSYLVANIA
CURRIER AND IVES

CHIEF LOGAN'S LAMENT

Logan, Chief of the Mingos, 1774

PAINTING ABOVE:
INDIAN HORSEMANSHIP
GEORGE CATLIN (1796-1872)

I appeal to any white man to say, if ever he entered Logan's cabin hungry, and he gave him not meat: if ever he came cold and naked, and he cloathed him not. During the course of the last long and bloody war Logan remained idle in his cabin, an advocate for peace. Such was my love for the whites, that my countrymen pointed as they passed, and said, "Logan is the friend of white man." I had even thought to have lived with you, but for the injuries of one man. Colonel Cresap, the last spring, in cold blood, and unprovoked, murdered all the relations of Logan, not even sparing my women and children. There runs not a drop of my blood in the veins of any living creature. This called on me for revenge. I have sought it: I have killed many: I have fully glutted my vengeance: for my country I rejoice at the beams of peace. But do not harbour a thought that mine is the joy of fear. Logan never felt fear. He will not turn on his heel to save his life. Who is there to mourn for Logan?—Not one.

Chief Logan was leader of the Mingo Indians of the Ohio River Valley in the late 1700s. Logan had been a friend to white settlers, but after a soldier murdered all of his family, he led a brutal attack against an English settlement. When his forces were defeated, Logan refused to surrender; instead, he sent this speech to Lord Dunmore, governor of Virginia. Thomas Jefferson took note of Logan's eloquent words, as did many other Americans who were moved for the first time to acknowledge the humanity of the Native American people.

138 AN INHERITANCE OF EMPATHY

from A CENTURY OF DISHONOR

Helen Hunt Jackson, 1881

However great perplexity and difficulty there may be in the details of any and every plan possible for doing at this late day anything like justice to the Indian, however hard it may be for good statesmen and good men to agree upon the things that ought to be done, there certainly is, or ought to be, no perplexity whatever, no difficulty whatever, in agreeing upon certain things that ought not to be done, and which must cease to be done before the first steps can be taken toward righting the wrongs, curing the ills, and wiping out the disgrace to us of the present condition of our Indians.

Cheating, robbing, breaking promises—these three are clearly things which must cease to be done. One more thing, also, and that is the refusal of the protection of the law to the Indian's rights of property, "of life, liberty, and the pursuit of happiness."

When these four things have ceased to be done, time, statesmanship, philanthropy, and Christianity can slowly and surely do the rest. Till these four things have ceased to be done, statesmanship and philanthropy alike must work in vain, and even Christianity can reap but a small harvest.

Helen Hunt Jackson began her life much as any other woman of her day. Born in Amherst, Massachusetts, in 1830, she married young, had two sons, and devoted her energies to the roles of wife and mother. Tragedy changed the course of her life, however; by 1865 she had lost her husband and both of her sons and turned to writing poetry and magazine articles to take her mind off her grief. She was remarried and living in Colorado Springs when she heard a lecture on the mistreatment of Native Americans. Jackson then undertook a course of detailed research into the issue, culminating in A Century of Dishonor, *which she sent to every member of Congress. In the paper, Jackson urged the government to halt the exploitation and oppression of the native people.*

PAINTING RIGHT:
YOUNG OMAHA, WAR EAGLE, LITTLE MISSOURI, AND PAWNEES, 1831
CHARLES BIRD KING
(1785-1862)
OIL ON CANVAS
NATIONAL MUSEUM OF AMERICAN ART

THE NEW COLOSSUS

Emma Lazarus

Not like the brazen giant of Greek fame,
　　With conquering limbs astride from land to land;
　　Here at our sea-washed, sunset gates shall stand
A mighty woman with a torch, whose flame
Is the imprisoned lightning, and her name
Mother of Exiles. From her beacon-hand
Glows world-wide welcome; her mild eyes command
The air-bridged harbor that twin cities frame.

"Keep, ancient lands, your storied pomp!" cries she
With silent lips. "Give me your tired, your poor,
Your huddled masses yearning to breathe free,
The wretched refuse of your teeming shore.
Send these, the homeless, tempest-tost to me,
I lift my lamp beside the golden door!"

The Statue of Liberty was unveiled and dedicated by President Grover Cleveland on October 28, 1886, at a ceremony on Bedloe's Island off the coast of New York City. The copper statue, a gift from the French in honor of one hundred years of American independence, weighed 250 tons and stood 152 feet tall. The poem that we so closely associate with the Statue of Liberty, Emma Lazarus's "The New Colossus," did not play a part in the ceremony. Lazarus, a New York poet who published her first book at the age of eighteen, wrote the poem in 1883, but it was not until 1903 that it was placed on a plaque inside the entrance of the statue. Some Americans were reluctant to embrace the sentiments of Lazarus's poem, hesitant to embrace the world's "huddled masses."

It was not until 1945, when Americans could no longer deny the contribution that recent immigrants had made to their society or the pride they felt at being the refuge of displaced peoples from across the world, that "The New Colossus" took its rightful place just outside the entrance to the Statue of Liberty, announcing to all who enter that America cherishes its role as "the golden door."

from MEMORIAL: TO THE LEGISLATURE OF MASSACHUSETTS

Dorothea Lynde Dix, 1843

Men of Massachusetts, I beg, I implore, I demand, pity and protection, for these of my suffering, outraged sex!—Fathers, Husbands, Brothers, I would supplicate you for this boon—but what do I say? I dishonor you, divest you at once of christianity and humanity—does this appeal imply distrust. If it comes burthened with a doubt of your righteousness in this Legislation, then blot it out; while I declare confidence in your honor, not less than your humanity. Here you will put away the cold, calculating spirit of selfishness and self-seeking; lay off the armor of local strife and political opposition; here and now, for once, forgetful of the earthly and perishable, come up to these halls and consecrate them with one heart and one mind to works of righteousness and just judgment. Become the benefactors of your race, the just guardians of the solemn rights you hold in trust. Raise up the fallen; succor the desolate; restore the outcast; defend the helpless; and for your eternal and great reward, receive the benediction. . . . "Well done, good and faithful servants, become rulers over many things!"

But, gentlemen, I do not come to quicken your sensibilities into short-lived action, to pour forth passionate exclamation, nor yet to move your indignation against those, whose misfortune, not fault, it surely is to hold in charge these poor demented creatures, and whose whole of domestic economy, or prison discipline, is absolutely overthrown by such proximity of conflicting circumstances, and opposite conditions of mind and character. . . .

While our *revised statutes* permit the incarceration of madmen and madwomen, epileptics and idiots in prisons, all responsible officers should, in ordinary justice, be exonerated from obligation to maintain prison discipline. And the fact is conclusive, if the injustice to prison officers is great, it is equally great towards prisoners; an additional penalty to a legal sentence pronounced in a Court of Justice, which might, we should think, in all the prisons we have visited, serve as a sound plea for false imprisonment. If reform is intended to be united with punishment, there never was a greater absurdity than to look for moral restoration under such circumstances; and if that is left out of view, we know no rendering of the law which sanctions such a cruel and oppressive aggravation of the circumstances of imprisonment, as to expose these prisoners day and night to the indescribable horrors of such association. . . .

It is not few, but many, it is not part but the whole, who bear unqualified testimony to this evil. A voice strong and deep comes up from every almshouse and prison in Massachusetts where the insane are or have been, protesting against such evils as have been illustrated in the preceding pages.

Gentlemen, I commit to you this sacred cause. Your action upon this subject will affect the present and future condition of hundreds and of thousands.

In this legislation, as in all things, may you exercise that "wisdom which is the breath of the power of God."

On March 28, 1841, Dorothea Dix, a substitute teacher at a Sunday school in an East Cambridge, Massachusetts, jail, discovered that among the incarcerated were several severely mentally ill inmates locked in tiny, filthy, unheated cells. The thirty-nine-year-old Dix, moved by the sight of these prisoners, launched a one-woman crusade to improve their situation. She singlehandedly conducted a survey of all public jails in Massachusetts, the result of which was her Memorial to the state legislature. At first her cries for reform were given little notice, but she was unrelenting until a bill was passed to improve the care of the mentally ill in Massachusetts. Dix then carried her message to other states, with much success. In 1841, when she began, there were eleven mental hospitals in the United States, and most persons with mental illness were housed and treated worse than the most violent criminals; by 1880 there were 123 hospitals, and the American public had begun to acknowledge their responsibility to care for the mentally ill.

PORTRAIT LEFT:
JANE ADDAMS (1860-1935)
GEORGE DE FOREST BRUSH
(1855-1941)
OIL ON CANVAS
NATIONAL PORTRAIT GALLERY
SMITHSONIAN INSTITUTION

Jane Addams was awarded the Nobel Prize in 1931 for her work to promote world peace. As founder of the Women's International League for Peace and Freedom, she worked tirelessly after World War I to promote the social justice and understanding that would help the world avoid future wars. During the war, Addams had won praise from some and disapproval from many for her continued stand against war of any kind, but public opinion of her work never swayed her from her purpose—to do what she could to achieve a lasting peace in the world. Addams's work was as practical as it was idealistic. In Chicago in the late 1880s, Addams had founded Hull House, a settlement house in the city's poorest neighborhood which served as a center for education, job training, and recreation for the community. Hull House was the first of many settlement houses in the United States, all organized and run by people with a strong desire to do something to help the less privileged members of society. Addams used the recognition she received for the success of Hull House to launch a campaign of writing and speaking aimed at advancing the cause of social justice in America. For almost one hundred years, the work of Jane Addams has been a model, and an inspiration, for the countless men and women who work to make life better for all Americans.

PHOTOGRAPH ABOVE:
PEACE ACTIVISTS, WWI
FPG INTERNATIONAL

I SHALL NOT PASS AGAIN THIS WAY

Author unknown

The bread that bringeth strength I want to give,
The water pure that bids the thirsty live:
I want to help the failing day by day;
I'm sure I shall not pass again this way.

I want to give the oil of joy for tears,
The faith to conquer crowding doubts and fears.
Beauty for ashes may I give alway:
I'm sure I shall not pass again this way.

I want to give some measure running o'er,
And into angry hearts I want to pour
The answer soft that turneth wrath away;
I'm sure I shall not pass again this way.

I want to give to others hope and faith,
I want to do all that the Master saith;
I want to live aright from day to day;
I'm sure I shall not pass again this way.

JOLLY FLATBOATMEN IN PORT, 1857
GEORGE CALEB BINGHAM (1811-1879)
OIL ON CANVAS
46¼ X 69 INCHES
THE ST. LOUIS ART MUSEUM
MUSEUM PURCHASE
ST. LOUIS, MISSOURI

THE QUEST FOR UNITY

Let us discard all this quibbling about this man and the other man, this race and that race. . . . Let us discard all these things, and unite as one people throughout this land, until we shall once more stand up declaring that all men are created equal.

Abraham Lincoln

A HOUSE DIVIDED

Abraham Lincoln, 1858

If we could first know where we are, and whither we are tending, we could better judge what to do, and how to do it. We are now far into the fifth year since a policy was initiated with the avowed object and confident promise of putting an end to slavery agitation. Under the operation of that policy that agitation has not only not ceased, but has constantly augmented. In my opinion, it will not cease until a crisis shall have been reached and passed. "A house divided against itself can not stand." I believe this Government cannot endure permanently half slave and half free. I do not expect the Union to be dissolved—I do not expect the house to fall— but I do expect it will cease to be divided. It will become all one thing, or all the other. Either the opponents of slavery will arrest the further spread of it, and place it where the public mind shall rest in the belief that it is in course of ultimate extinction; or its advocates will push it forward till it shall become alike lawful in all the States, old as well as new, North as well as South. . . . Our cause, then, must be intrusted to, and conducted by, its own undoubted friends—those whose hands are free, whose hearts are in the work, who do care for the result. Two years ago the Republicans of the nation mustered over thirteen hundred thousand strong. We did this under the single impulse of resistance to a common danger, with every external circumstance against us. Of strange, discordant, and even hostile elements, we gathered from the four winds, and formed and fought the battle through, under the constant hot fire of a disciplined, proud, and pampered enemy. Did we brave all then to falter now?—now, when that same enemy is wavering, dissevered, and belligerent? The result is not doubtful. We shall not fail—if we stand firm, we shall not fail. Wise counsels may accelerate or mistakes delay it, but, sooner or later, the victory is sure to come.

There has been perhaps no more staunch protector of our Union than President Abraham Lincoln, who—at a time when passions were running high all across the nation, a time when many had lost sight of the fact that the word "Union" truly referred to all the United States of America, North and South— kept his sacred pledge to maintain the great Union his forefathers had begun. We are a nation of many regions, many ideologies, many races, many religions, but as the example of President Lincoln will always remind us, we are above all one nation, with greater bonds to hold us together than differences to break us apart.

PAINTING ABOVE:
CAPITOL BUILDING
WASHINGTON, D.C.,
ABOUT 1830

THE BETTER ANGELS OF OUR NATURE
Abraham Lincoln, 1861, from the first Inaugural Address

In *your* hands, my dissatisfied fellow-countrymen, and not in *mine*, is the momentous issue of civil war. The Government will not assail *you*. You can have no conflict without being yourselves the aggressors. *You* have no oath registered in heaven to destroy the Government, while *I* shall have the most solemn one to "preserve, protect, and defend it." I am loath to close. We are not enemies, but friends. We must not be enemies. Though passion may have strained it must not break our bonds of affection. The mystic chords of memory, stretching from every battlefield and patriot grave to every living heart and hearthstone all over this broad land, will yet swell the chorus of the Union, when again touched, as surely they will be, by the better angels of our nature.

from A SPEECH TO THE AMERICAN ANTI-SLAVERY SOCIETY

Frederick Douglass, 1865

Slavery is not abolished until the black man has the ballot. While the Legislatures of the South retain the right to pass laws making any discrimination between black and white, slavery still lives there. As Edmund Quincy once said, "While the word 'white' is on the statute-book of Massachusetts, Massachusetts is a slave State. While a black man can be turned out of a car in Massachusetts, Massachusetts is a slave State. While a slave can be taken from old Massachusetts, Massachusetts is a slave State." That is what I heard Edmund Quincy say twenty-three or twenty-four years ago. I never forget such a thing. Now, while the black man can be denied a vote, while the Legislatures of the South can take from him the right to keep and bear arms, as they can—they would not allow a Negro to walk with a cane where I came from, they would not allow five of them to assemble together—the work of the Abolitionists is not finished. . . . Where shall the black man look for support, my friends, if the American Anti-Slavery Society fails him? From whence shall we expect a certain sound from the trumpet of freedom, when the old pioneer, when this Society that has survived mobs, and martyrdom, and the combined efforts of the priest-craft and state-craft to suppress it, shall at once subside, on the mere intimation that the Constitution has been amended, so that neither slavery nor involuntary servitude shall hereafter be allowed in this land? . . . Slavery has been fruitful in giving itself names. It has been called "the peculiar institution," "the social system," and the "impediment," as it was called by the General conference of the Methodist Episcopal Church. It has been called a great many names, and it will call itself by yet another name; and you and I and all of us had better wait and see what new form this old monster will assume, in what new skin this old snake will come forth.

Frederick Douglass urged the American Anti-Slavery Society not to disband simply because the war was won and the Thirteenth Amendment, outlawing slavery, was approved. He warned that discrimination would persist despite the laws of the land, and that true unity of the black and white peoples of America would take time, hard work, and a true commitment to equality on the part of all Americans.

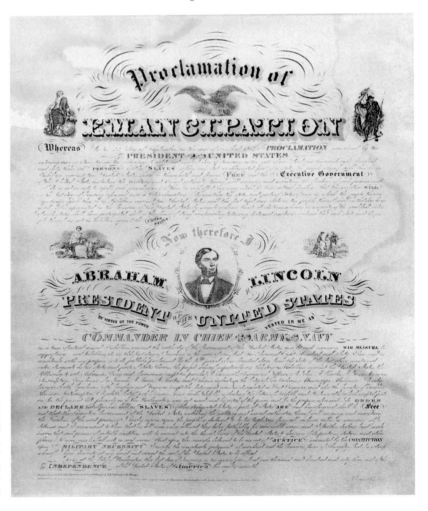

RIGHT:
ABRAHAM LINCOLN AND THE EMANCIPATION PROCLAMATION
ALBERT KIDDER
CHARLES SHOBER LITHOGRAPHY COMPANY
LITHOGRAPH
NATIONAL PORTRAIT GALLERY
SMITHSONIAN INSTITUTION

THE ORATION

Chief Seattle, 1854

Yonder sky that has wept tears of compassion upon my people for centuries untold, and which to us appears changeless and eternal, may change. Today is fair. Tomorrow it may be overcast with clouds. My words are like the stars that never change. Whatever Seattle says the great chief at Washington can rely upon with as much certainty as he can upon the return of the sun or the seasons. . . .

There was a time when our people covered the land as the waves of a wind-ruffled sea cover its shell paved floor, but that time long since passed away with the greatness of tribes that are now but a mournful memory. I will not dwell on, nor mourn over, our untimely decay, nor reproach my paleface brothers with hastening it as we too may have been somewhat to blame. . . .

A few more moons. A few more winters—and not one of the descendants of the mighty hosts that once moved over this broad land or lived in happy homes, protected by the Great Spirit, will remain to mourn over the graves of a people—once more powerful and hopeful than yours. But why should I mourn at the untimely fate of my people? Tribe follows tribe, and nation follows nation, like the waves of the sea. It is the order of nature, and regret is useless. Your time of decay may be distant, but it will surely come, for even the White Man whose God walked and talked with him as friend with friend, cannot be exempt from the common destiny. We may be brothers after all. We will see.

We will ponder your proposition and when we decide we will let you know. But should we accept it, I here and now make this condition that we will not be denied the privilege without molestation of visiting at any time the tombs of our ancestors, friends and children. Every part of this soil is sacred in the estimation of my people. Every hillside, every valley, every plain and grove, has been hallowed by some sad or happy event in days long vanished. Even the rocks, which seem to be dumb and dead as they swelter in the sun along the silent shore, thrill with memories of stirring events connected with the lives of my people, and the very dust upon which you now stand responds more lovingly to their footsteps than to yours, because it is rich with the blood of our ancestors and our bare feet are conscious of the sympathetic touch. Our departed braves, fond mothers, glad, happy-hearted maidens, and even the little children who lived here and rejoiced here for brief season, will love these somber solitudes and at eventide they greet shadowy returning spirits. And when the last Red Man shall have perished, and the memory of my tribe shall have become a myth among the White Men, these shores will swarm with the invisible dead of my tribe, and when your children's children think themselves alone in the field, the store, the shop, upon the highway, or in the silence of the pathless woods, they will not be alone. In all the earth there is no place dedicated to solitude. At night when the streets of your cities and villages are silent and you think them deserted, they will throng with the returning hosts that once filled them and still love this beautiful land. The White Man will never be alone.

Let him be just and deal kindly with my people, for the dead are not powerless. Dead, did I say? There is no death, only a change of worlds.

Chief Seattle was the leader of six Native American tribes in the Pacific Northwest. His Oration was delivered in response to an offer by the American government to buy his people's land and move them to a reservation. His words, considered the symbolic final acceptance of the Native Americans of the loss of their land, are important not as a statement of defeat but as an articulate, moving explanation of his view of the world and the way of life of his people. Seattle told his audience that day in 1854 that no matter how our lives and our land change, the past is always with us; his oration is a valuable part of our national heritage, for it is a reminder that while we must always seek unity, we must also always allow for diversity.

from A LETTER FROM ABIGAIL TO JOHN ADAMS

March 31, 1776

I long to hear that you have declared an independancy—and by the way in the new Code of Laws which I suppose it will be necessary for you to make I desire you would Remember the Ladies, and be more generous and favourable to them than your ancestors. Do not put such unlimited power into the hands of the Husbands. Remember all Men would be tyrants if they could. If perticuliar care and attention is not paid to the Ladies we are determined to foment a Rebelion, and will not hold ourselves bound by any Laws in which we have no voice, or Representation.

Long before the issue of women's rights was publicly debated in America, Abigail Adams urged her husband John to give consideration to the equal rights of female Americans when formulating the laws of the new United States of America. The excerpt at left comes from a letter written to Mr. Adams as he debated the question of independence as a member of the Continental Congress. Abigail Adams, intelligent, educated, and free-thinking, got no more than a joking response from her husband, who, like the majority of the male leaders of his day, considered independence and equality to be words that applied to men, not women. Time, however, would prove Abigail Adams correct; before the United States could lay true claim to being a nation founded on the values of liberty and equality, its national understanding of those words would need to be expanded to include both halves of the population.

SENECA FALLS DECLARATION OF SENTIMENTS AND RESOLUTIONS
1848

When, in the course of human events, it becomes necessary for one portion of the family of man to assume among the people of the earth a position different from that which they have hitherto occupied, but one to which the laws of nature and of nature's God entitle them, a decent respect to the opinions of mankind requires that they should declare the causes that impel them to such a course.

We hold these truths to be self-evident: that all men and women are created equal; that they are endowed by their Creator with certain inalienable rights; that among these are life, liberty, and the pursuit of happiness; that to secure these rights governments are instituted, deriving their just powers from the consent of the governed.—Whenever any form of Government becomes destructive of these ends, it is the right of those who suffer from it to refuse allegiance to it, and to insist upon the institution of a new government, laying its foundation on such principles, and organizing its powers in such form as to them shall seem most likely to effect their safety and happiness. . . .

Resolved, That all laws which prevent women from occupying such a station in society as her conscience shall dictate, or which place her in a position inferior to that of man, are contrary to the great precept of nature, and therefore of no force or authority. . . .

Resolved, That the women of this country ought to be enlightened in regard to the laws under which they live, that they may no longer publish their degradation, by declaring themselves satisfied with their present position, nor their ignorance, by asserting that they have all the rights they want. . . .

Resolved, That it is the duty of the women of this country to secure to themselves their sacred right to the elective franchise. . . .

Resolved, therefore, That, being invested by the Creator with the same capabilities, and the same consciousness of responsibility for their exercise, it is demonstrably the right and duty of woman, equally with man, to promote every righteous cause, by every righteous means; and especially in regard to the great subjects of morals and religion, it is self-evidently her right to participate with her brother in teaching them, both in private and in public, by writing and by speaking, by any instrumentalities proper to be used, and in any assemblies proper to be held; and this being a self-evident truth, growing out of the divinely implanted principles of human nature, any custom or authority adverse to it, whether modern or wearing the hoary sanction of antiquity, is to be regarded as self-evident falsehood, and at war with the interests of mankind.

Nearly seventy-five years after Abigail Adams urged her husband to consider granting equal rights to women when drawing up the laws of the nation, little progress had been made toward that end. Women in mid-nineteenth-century America had few of the rights and privileges of their male counterparts. The convention at Seneca Falls, New York, was organized by Elizabeth Cady Stanton; its goal was to use the language of the founding fathers to express the dissatisfaction of the nation's women. The Declaration of Sentiments, taking its form from the Declaration of Independence, was not well-received by the general American public, many of whom saw no need for women's rights. But the chorus of voices was growing and would continue to grow as the decades passed.

Thou, too, sail on, O Ship of State!
Sail on, O Union, strong and great!
Humanity with all its fears,
With all the hopes of future years,
Is hanging breathless on thy fate!

Henry Wadsworth Longfellow
from "The Building of the Ship"

No more shall the war cry sever,
    Or the winding rivers be red;
They banish our anger forever
    When they laurel the graves of our dead!
        Under the sod and the dew,
            Waiting the judgment day;—
        Love and tears for the Blue,
            Tears and love for the Gray.

Francis Miles Finch
from "The Blue and the Gray"

PHOTOGRAPH ABOVE:
PRESIDENTIAL CAMPAIGN BUTTON, 1948

When peace has been broken anywhere, the peace of all countries everywhere is in danger.

Franklin Delano Roosevelt
Fireside Chat
September 1939

POSTCARD ABOVE:
GEORGE WASHINGTON'S BIRTHDAY

Let us discard all this quibbling about this man and the other man, this race and that race. . . . Let us discard all these things, and unite as one people throughout this land, until we shall once more stand up declaring that all men are created equal.

Abraham Lincoln

This dust was once the man,
Gentle, plain, just and resolute, under whose cautious hand,
Against the foulest crime in history known in any land or age,
Was saved the Union of these States.

Walt Whitman
from "This Dust Was Once the Man"

LEFT:
WAGON TRAIN TO THE WEST
LIBRARY OF CONGRESS

It is not merely for today but for all time to come that we should perpetuate for our children's children that great and free government which we have enjoyed all our lives. I beg you to remember this, not merely for my sake, but for yours. I happen, temporarily, to occupy the White House. I am a living witness that any one of your children may look to come here as my father's child has. It is in order that each one of you may have, through this free government which we have enjoyed, an open field and a fair chance for your industry, enterprise, and intelligence, that you may all have equal privileges in the race of life, with all its desirable human aspirations. It is for this the struggle should be maintained that we may not lose our birthright—not only for one, but for two or three years. The nation is worth fighting for to secure such an inestimable jewel.

Abraham Lincoln

DUTY, HONOR, COUNTRY

General Douglas MacArthur, 1962

In twenty campaigns, on a hundred battlefields, around a thousand campfires, I have witnessed that enduring fortitude, that patriotic self-abnegation, and that invincible determination which have carved his statue in the hearts of his people.

As I listened to those songs of the glee club, in memory's eye I could see those staggering columns of the First World War, bending under soggy packs, on many a weary march from dripping dusk to drizzling dawn. . . . I do not know the dignity of their birth but I do know the glory of their death. They died unquestioning, uncomplaining, with faith in their hearts, and on their lips the hope that we would go on to victory. Always for them—Duty-Honor-Country; always their blood and sweat and tears as we sought the way and the light and the truth. . . .

The shadows are lengthening for me. The twilight is here. My days of old have vanished tone and tint; they have gone glimmering through the dreams of things that were. Their memory is one of wondrous beauty, watered by tears, and coaxed and caressed by the smiles of yesterday. . . .

Today marks my final roll call with you, but I want you to know that when I cross the river my last conscious thought will be The Corps—and The Corps—and The Corps—and The Corps.

I bid you farewell.

THE TORCH IS PASSED

John F. Kennedy, Inaugural Address, 1961

Man holds in his mortal hands the power to abolish all forms of human poverty and all forms of human life. And yet the same revolutionary beliefs for which our forebears fought are still at issue around the globe—the belief that the rights of man come not from the generosity of the state but from the hand of God.

We dare not forget today we are the heirs of that first revolution. Let the word go forth from this time and place, to friend and foe alike, that the torch has been passed to a new generation of Americans—born in this century, tempered by war, disciplined by a hard and bitter peace, proud of our ancient heritage—and unwilling to witness or permit the slow undoing of those human rights to which this nation has always been committed, and to which we are committed today at home and around the world.

Let every nation know, whether it wishes us well or ill, that we shall pay any price, bear any burden, meet any hardship, support any friend, oppose any foe to assure the survival and the success of liberty.

This much we pledge—and more. . . .

In the long history of the world, only a few generations have been granted the role of defending freedom in its hour of maximum danger. I do not shrink from this responsibility—I welcome it. I do not believe that any of us would exchange places with any other people or any other generation. The energy, the faith, the devotion which we bring to this endeavor will light our country and all who serve it—and the glow from that fire can truly light the world.

And so, my fellow Americans: ask not what your country can do for you—ask what you can do for your country.

My fellow citizens of the world: ask not what America will do for you, but what together we can do for the freedom of man.

Finally, whether you are citizens of America or citizens of the world, ask of us here the same high standards of strength and sacrifice which we ask of you. With a good conscience our only sure reward, with history the final judge of our deeds, let us go forth to lead the land we love, asking His blessing and His help, but knowing that here on earth God's work must truly be our own.

The quest for unity in America was only just begun when the victory at Yorktown completed the war for independence from Great Britain. Through the years that have followed, Americans have struggled to achieve a unified vision and purpose, and each new day has brought new challenges and new obstacles. In modern times, true unity involves not just unity among the people and regions of our own nation, but the unity of the nations of the world in the search for liberty, equality, and peace. Leaders like General MacArthur, who fought for peace and freedom in battles on both sides of the world, and President John Kennedy, who called upon all Americans to work together to achieve the "freedom of man," have set an example that all Americans can follow. The quest for unity, at home and abroad, is a never-ending one and demands our complete courage and commitment.

"The American Idea" is an unfinished article written by Theodore H. White to commemorate the two-hundredth anniversary of the United States Constitution. His words remind us that what holds us together as a nation is our common heritage—not a racial, ethnic, or religious heritage, but a heritage of ideas and belief. American unity is by definition inclusive; we trace our roots to all corners of the world. But while our pasts are a picture of diversity, we face the challenges of today and of the future as one people, drawing on the rich heritage of America for guidance and inspiration.

PHOTOGRAPH ABOVE:
THE FLAG OF THE UNITED STATES THAT FLEW OVER FORT MCHENRY IN 1814 AND INSPIRED FRANCIS SCOTT KEY TO WRITE "THE STAR SPANGLED BANNER"
ARMED FORCES HISTORY DIVISION
MUSEUM OF AMERICAN HISTORY
SMITHSONIAN INSTITUTION

THE AMERICAN IDEA

Theodore H. White, 1986

The idea was there at the very beginning, well before Thomas Jefferson put it into words—and the idea rang the call.

Jefferson himself could not have imagined the reach of his call across the world in time to come when he wrote:

"We hold these truths to be self-evident, that all men are created equal, that they are endowed by their Creator with certain unalienable rights, that among these are life, liberty and the pursuit of happiness."

But over the next two centuries the call would reach the potato patches of Ireland, the ghettoes of Europe, the paddyfields of China, stirring farmers to leave their lands and townsmen their trades and thus unsettling all traditional civilizations.

It is the call from Thomas Jefferson, embodied in the great statue that looks down the Narrows of New York Harbor, and in the immigrants who answered the call, that we now celebrate.

Some of the first European Americans had come to the new continent to worship God in their own way, others to seek their fortunes. But over a century-and-a-half, the new world changed those Europeans, above all the Englishmen who had come to North America. Neither King nor Court nor church could stretch over the ocean to the wild continent. To survive, the first emigrants had to learn to govern themselves. But the freedom of the wilderness whetted their appetites for more freedoms. By the time Jefferson drafted his call, men were in the field fighting for those new-learned freedoms, killing and being killed by English soldiers, the best-trained troops in the world, supplied by the world's greatest navy. Only something worth dying for could unite American volunteers and keep them in the field—a stated cause, a flag, a nation they could call their own.

When, on the Fourth of July, 1776, the colonial leaders who had been meeting as a Continental Congress in Philadelphia voted to approve Jefferson's Declaration of Independence, it was not puffed-up rhetoric for them to pledge to each other "our lives, our fortunes and our sacred honor." Unless their new "United States of America" won the war, the Congressmen would be judged traitors as relentlessly as would the irregulars-under-arms in the field. And all knew what English law allowed in the case of a traitor. The victim could be partly strangled; drawn, or disemboweled, while still alive, his entrails then burned and his body quartered.

The new Americans were tough men fighting for a very tough idea. How they won their battle is a story for the schoolbooks, studied by scholars, wrapped in myths by historians and poets.

But what is most important is the story of the idea that made them into a nation, the idea that had an explosive power undreamed of in 1776.

All other nations had come into being among people whose families had lived for time out of mind on the same land where they were born. Englishmen are English, Frenchmen are French, Chinese are Chinese, while their governments come and go; their national states can be torn apart and remade without losing their nationhood. But Americans are a nation born of an idea; not the place, but the idea, created the United States Government.

INDEX